# Changed Forever

*101 Life Changing Verses and Commentary*
*To Transform Your Mind and Soul*

Dr. JAMES A. CARTER

authorHOUSE®

AuthorHouse™
1663 Liberty Drive
Bloomington, IN 47403
www.authorhouse.com
Phone: 1-800-839-8640

Published by AuthorHouse 2/8/2013

ISBN: 978-1-4817-0872-2 (sc)
ISBN: 978-1-4817-0870-8 (hc)
ISBN: 978-1-4817-0871-5 (e)

Library of Congress Control Number: 2013900937

# About the Author

Dr. James A. Carter has been an ordained minister since 1986. He has held numerous positions within the church, including youth pastor, music minister, associate pastor and senior pastor.

Dr. Carter's business career includes working as a psychologist, serving as warden for several state and local prison systems, and as superintendent for a state mental health hospital. He is a nationally recognized speaker and author on the subjects of Christian Living, Corrections, and Mental Health. He holds a Ph.D. in Counseling Psychology and a B.S. and M.S. in Public Administration.

Dr. Carter is married to his lovely wife Sherry. They are parents to three adult children, Carissa Danielle, Douglas Lee, and John Michael. The Carters share their home with their standard poodle named Sadie.

# Dedication

I give glory and honor to my Lord and Savior Jesus Christ. Without Him I would be lost, separated from His love, without a promise of eternal life with my heavenly Father. I thank Him for the wisdom and strength to write this book.

I thank my beautiful wife Sherry who has been a constant source of encouragement, love, and persistence. She portrays the characteristics of a godly woman every day. She has been the inspiration for this project and my constant supporter. It was through her love, encouragement, and determination that this book was completed. We are both blessed with the support of her sons, Douglas and John.

I appreciate my daughter, Carissa, who has been a blessing from the Lord for twenty-one years. I pray that God will continue to bless her every day as she grows in the Lord and serves Him daily. Many of my stories were inspired by watching her grow up into an amazing young woman.

I also thank my brother, sisters, and parents for their continued love and support. I am sure many of their gray hairs are from seeking the Lord on my behalf. I love them all and thank God that they know Jesus as their Lord and Savior. I know we will spend eternity together worshipping our heavenly Father in our glorified bodies. (All of you know we need them!)

# Table of Contents

# Introduction

We all say we can't learn scripture. It's just too hard, it takes too long, and we get discouraged. My question is how can we learn anything else we know? Phone numbers, sport statistics, recipes, and songs? How many have sat down with a song list and tried to learn all of their favorites? Or have tried to learn every statistical fact about their favorite sports teams?

Find people who have been in the church for a long period of time and ask them if they sat down with the hymnal to learn all of the words to the great hymns. I'm pretty sure they would say they have not. Well, how do they know the words to so many of the glorious life changing hymns? It's called repetition.

When we learn scriptures it is not like we will sit down and "cram" like we were studying for a final exam. When students memorize material just for a test, that knowledge does not stay with them very long. Why? First of all, they are doing it out of necessity for a temporal purpose, to get a good grade. Secondly, the material did not make an impact on their lives. Thirdly, after the test they did not return to the subject matter.

What is the best way to learn scripture so it becomes part of your life? Let me use this illustration. Over the years I have enjoyed jogging. Okay, maybe not totally enjoyed it, but I knew the necessity of it to keep my weight down, to be healthier, and stay in my existing wardrobe. As I jogged, I would listen to fast beat, up tempo secular music to keep me going. I told myself that although it was secular music I was only listening for the up tempo beat and to keep me at the right jogging pace. I had no desire to learn the words of the music. As a matter of fact, I wished there were no words to the music. However, as I continued to run listening to the secular music, the words began to permeate my mind. I began to notice that I would start saying the words and singing the words as I jogged. Then the words came into my thoughts during the day. I realized that even though I did not set out to learn these songs (was even dead set against learning the words), I in actuality learned the songs and they were entering my thoughts throughout the day. If a situation happened during the day my first thoughts to respond came from these secular songs! I should be seeking answers from the Word of God! So whatever you feed your spirit the most is what will be a part of your daily living.

Feed your mind these scriptures daily, not because you want to memorize them but because you will be **Changed Forever!** Read these scriptures, study them, make a CD of you reading these scriptures daily, and you will do two things! You will learn the scriptures so well you will begin to quote them, know them inside and out, and they will become a part of you. Secondly, when the scriptures become a part of you, quote them to your selfish man, quote them to Satan in times of temptation, quote them for encouragement and victory, and **your life will be CHANGED FOREVER!** Unlike any secular knowledge that may benefit you, the Word of God will be as fresh as air is to our lungs, as water is to our bodies and food to a starving man!

At this time you may still doubt whether you can learn the scriptures adequately enough to be able to witness, minister to those hurting, or for self-preservation. I know you can! Let me tell you about a special man that I had the privilege of meeting and knowing on a personal level. His name was Rev. J.G. Hall, and he was a professor of mine in college. Not only was he a professor, he was an author, preacher, evangelist, dispensationalist, and a great man of God. Not only did I learn the Word of God under his leadership but I learned what it meant to be a true man of God. Rev. Hall was a very quiet, humble man. Yet when in the pulpit he spoke the Word of God with authority, never turning from the spiritual truths that needed to be taught, and always preaching repentance, grace, and sanctification. I had the pleasure of sitting in many of his services but I was especially blessed when he came to a church where I was an associate pastor. He stayed in my home and we talked about the things of God for what seemed like an eternity. I forgot to mention the most amazing, unbelievable part of his ministry — Rev. Hall had learned the entire Bible word for word, forward and backward! As he taught in his services people would ask him questions and he would begin to quote the scripture by memory. No matter what book, verse, or testament, he could start and not stop until he proved the authority of God's Word on the subject.

As Rev. Hall and I were sitting in my living room late one evening, I asked him how he was able to memorize the entire Bible, cover to cover. His answer changed my life and challenged me even until this very day. He stated, *"What else is there?"* This is the life-giving, life-changing Word of the Almighty God, and He gave it to us as a beacon in a dark world. I did not set out to memorize the Word of God; I set out to learn it, to meditate upon it, to digest it and to cradle it in the very depths of my soul. I hunger for the Word of God just as I do any other life sustaining element of my life. Air, water, food, the Word of God—they all are needed to survive and to live. Only the Word of God gives everlasting life and is not as temporal as the other items mentioned. Wow! Rev. Hall went on to say, "I know it and can quote it because I have stayed in the Word of God every day. I long for it and know that no matter how many times I read it and digest it, God uses it to change my life and continues the work He has started in me."

So if a man can learn the entire Bible from reading it, studying it and living it, then surely you and I can learn and live at least 101 verses in our lives on a daily basis. You may be thinking why should I learn and memorize scripture when I can go to my computer or other books and just look up what I need at that moment? What if we carried this train of thought to other areas of our lives? Why learn to drive a car when you can just look at the driver instructional manual when you need it? Why learn First Aid when you can just carry the manual and pull it out if you come across someone unconscious or not breathing? I could go on but I'm sure you understand my point. We need the Word of God in our hearts, minds, and souls so we can act immediately when life throws us a curveball. Because our mind controls our thoughts and our actions, we must rely on the Word of God to give us the directions of life at any moment. We must hide the Word of God in our lives so that we do not sin against God. ("I have hidden your word in my heart that I might not sin against you" Psalm 119:11.)

God has given us His anointed, life-giving Holy Word so that we may ***learn it, love it, and live it*** in Jesus' name!

# Different Techniques For Learning God's Word

Learning 101 verses sounds hard, right? But I know you can do it if you put your heart and mind to it! Ask God to be with you and to give you His strength to learn His Word. He wants you to know His Word and to live it. He will give you the strength and the brain power needed to learn the scriptures. In no time, you'll be looking for the next volume, Changed Forever 2 to learn.

Ask the Lord to help the Word of God to change you, transform you, and make you everything that He wants you to be. You never know, this may be the beginning of a new work or ministry that God wants to start in you!

I have several suggestions on how you can learn the Word of God and make it enjoyable and fun as well.

Create flash cards. Put the verse on one side of the card and put the entire scripture written out on the back of the card. Using index cards is great for this exercise. You can carry these cards with you anywhere and study every time you have a few minutes. At work, in lines at the store, waiting rooms, at home, at the park, at red lights, do not be afraid! You will find as you read the cards the Lord will begin hiding His Word in your heart.

You can't eat an elephant all at once. Do not try to learn 101 verses all at once. Pick up to ten and begin learning them. Or even start with one. Once you learn one verse you will see that you are able to learn scripture and you will be excited to move to the next verse. Learn the Word of God one bite at a time and you will soon be full of the Word of God and the wisdom of the Lord—and you will find yourself being changed forever!

Make learning scriptures a friendly challenge. Many people when trying to lose weight will get family members or friends to join them in a friendly competition. Having someone who is excited about the same goal that you have is great encouragement. Have a reward at each stage of the competition that will keep both of you willing to reach toward the goal of learning the Word of God. Ultimately, the greatest reward is hiding the Word of God in you heart and seeing your friend, family member, or friendly competitor changed by the almighty Word of God!

**Biblical Scholar?** I can say with all firmness and belief in my heart that if you learn 101 scriptures, you will know more scriptures and will have hidden more scriptures in your heart that anyone else you know! If you do not believe me then do your experiment. Ask one, ten or even 100 people how many scriptures they have hidden in their heart by learning them and can quote them to you. I will be shocked if anyone can quote more than ten scriptures to you correctly, the scripture and the verse (excluding the Lord's Prayer and Psalm 23). These two sections of scripture are admittedly widely known and many can quote them from childhood. That is one reason I did not include them in this book. The point is if you commit yourself and learn these very important 101 verses then your family, friends, church members, and those who are hurting and lost will come to you and see you as a biblical scholar! They will be amazed at your determination, dedication, and your love for the Word of God. You will have the power of our Heavenly Father to influence and change lives on a daily basis!

Use this book and create a Bible study. Study a verse each week and have everybody give an example of how the verse impacts them and their lives. Read the scripture, hear the examples, and take one week to learn the verse. The next week everyone should quote the verse learned and then work on the next verse. At the end of three months, the group should be able to quote twelve scriptures before moving to the next.

**Conclusion.** There are over 43,000 scriptures in the Word of God! Choosing the first 101 to learn is not easy. However, this is a starting point. I promise if you dedicate your life to learning His Word you will not want to stop with just 101 verses. You will be so inspired by His life-giving, life-changing Word that you will crave more of Him and become a life learner of the Word of God. I referenced Rev. Hall earlier. The key to learning the Word of God is in his answer when I asked how he learned the entire Bible by memory. His reply was, "*What else is there?*"

I agree 100% with his sentiment. What else will lift us when we are down? What else will give refuge when we are being attacked? Where else will one find the water that will quench every thirst? Where else can one find the answers to life beyond death? The Word of God is God, and as we hide it in our hearts, we are hiding God in our lives as well! In the Word of God, we have the greatest history book, love novel, suspense thriller, miracles and wonders, the answer to every problem we will come across, and meet the ultimate sacrifice anyone ever made. God gave His Son Jesus Christ to redeem mankind of its death-deserving sin. Jesus became the ultimate sacrifice so you and I could live with the Father and Him forever!

**Learn the Word! Love the Word! Live the Word!**

Be changed forever in Jesus name!

# Twelve Thinking Skills To Renew Your Mind

**Think with a right spirit within you.** After committing adultery with Bathsheba, David wrote Psalms 51 as a prayer of repentance unto God. He wrote, "Create in me a clean heart, O God, and renew a right spirit within me." To learn God's Word, you must dedicate yourself to maintaining a right spirit, a contrite spirit, which is a spirit after God's heart, a strong desire for the things of God and not the things of this world. Pray for a clean heart which implies to remove all impurities and filth, to clean all the corners, cobwebs and dust from every part of our heart. There cannot be "any hiding places" in our heart for undefiled things or areas of our life we are not willing to let go. God wants, expects and demands that we surrender all if we want His blessings.

**Think purposely.** You will put your time, money, and effort into what is important in your life. Be persistent in learning the Word of God! Make it a priority and focus on it as if your life depended on it—because it does! We are not promised a world where we will be fortunate enough to have a Bible all the time. If the Bible is removed physically, you will always have it hidden in your heart.

In the Word of God we read where four true friends wanted Jesus to heal their bedridden friend. However, they were not able to get to Jesus because of the crowds. Did they give up? No! They kept their focus and decided to go through the roof! Unorthodox yes, but very effective. Jesus stated that He had never seen such faith! Remain focused on your desire to learn God's Word and He will reward you mightily.

**Think with options in mind.** There is more than one way of completing a task. Do not let learning these verses become boring or mundane. Be creative! Change your tactics when trying to learn. Here are some ideas. Sometimes a change in scenery helps. Study in a new, refreshing spot or head to a lake, beach or secluded area. Ask a friend to join you. This would bring excitement to both of you in learning the scriptures and sharing your life experiences with each other. Create cue cards, use bible studies, record the verses and listen to them as you walk, jog, or work around the house. Keep studying His Word in fresh, exciting, and creative ways every day.

**Think responsibly.** I'm sure everyone would love to learn 101 verses in a month. I don't think so! Not most people! This is a spiritual marathon not a sprint. Set realistic goals for yourself. The goal will be different for everyone such as one verse a day, one verse a week, maybe even one verse a month for some. It doesn't matter as long as you're moving forward. The goal is to learn God's Word, get it into your heart and soul. Meditate on His Word and let it change you and transform you as you lock it in your heart.

**Think with discipline.** This project must be important to you—so important that you plan for your study time. Set a time every day that you can spend studying the scriptures, researching the scriptures, doing the hard work of learning the verse. You set a time to work, you set a time to sleep, you set a time to eat and be with family. Plan for your study time in God's Word. Commit it to your prayer time as the two go together nicely. If it's important to you then you will make the time to learn His word.

**Think outside of your little box.** You may have the plan all figured out. "I'm going to learn these verses to help me in my daily walk with the Lord." Or, "I'm learning the Word of God to get my family saved." These are very important reasons to study God's Word. But be prepared, God rarely leaves us in our comfort zone. When you commit to learning His Word and actually put forth the effort and accomplish learning His Word, God will open the doors of possibilities for you. God will begin to open doors you never even thought of being there for you. You may have a vision of where you want to end up, but God has a vision for your whole life as well! He will use you as much as you make yourself available to Him. Tell the Lord to use you however He desires and that you are willing to go.

**Think of your past to motivate your future.** Your past can be a powerful motivation. Past failures, disappointments, discouragements can motivate us to make necessary changes in our lives. Don't let these past memories haunt you, but use them to remind you of what you no longer desire to be. Positive memories of our past can also motivate us. No matter how good or wonderful things may have been, they can get better. The closer you move to God and grow in His Word, the more you will change into a different person. You will become a person who is full of God, His Word, His Spirit, His desire, His passion, His vision, and His priorities. Put off the old man and become the new creature that God desires you to be. Make room because the Holy Spirit is moving into your heart and He has a lot of cleaning to do!

**Think about pleasing your heavenly Father.** People in your immediate world may question your sudden devotion to learning God's Word. They may say that there are more important things you could do with your time. Do not listen to the conventional wisdom of this world. There may be other activities that would reward you with temporal things, but God's Word will bless you now and forever. "Do not grow weary in doing good" (Gal. 6:9).

**Think about challenging others.** You can take this opportunity of learning God's Word and challenge others with it. You can do this in many ways. Have one-on-one discussions with individuals who do not understand the scriptures or share your enthusiasm of the scriptures. Invite someone over for coffee, tea, or other beverage and open the bread of life with them. You could start a neighborhood study club. Invite neighbors and share your love of the Word of God. Share your testimony with them and show them how God's love can change their lives forever as well.

Take the verses you are learning and email them to family, friends, or loved ones. Let them know that God is doing a mighty work in your life and you want them to experience the life changing power of God as well. These ideas are only a few ways that you can challenge people to read and learn the Word of God.

Post a verse a week in your yard. You will bless others and they will begin to look forward to seeing what verse you put up next.

**Think with generosity.** Always have your heart open to ways that you can give to His world. We are not to be of the world, but we should give to the world that they may see and receive Christ. As you study the scriptures in this book you will find yourself desiring to make a greater impact in the world for Christ. Christ says in the great commission to "go unto all the world…" He simply says go without giving you all of the details. Once He sees that you are faithful to go, He will fill in the rest of the blanks as you go. Go and teach others about Christ and help them escape the death of sin and hell.

**Think and study to show yourself approved.** Think, study, pray, seek, fast, be prepared in season and out of season. You're in this to please God not man. What starts as simply wanting to learn a few scriptures could very well end up with being a ministry, a calling, a purpose. A God-given vision! All I know is if you prepare yourself God will use you. The greater the sacrifice, the greater the reward will be.

**"As a man thinketh in his heart, so is he!" Proverbs 23:7.** If you take in garbage long enough you become a garbage can! Protect yourself from the garbage of the world and from negative family members and friends. Philippians 4:8 tells us to think on things that are true, noble, just, pure, lovely, good report, virtuous, and praiseworthy.

Now that you have made the decision to learn the Word of God do not let others dump on you, speak to you words of discouragement, words of deception, lies or anything that is not of God. Protect your mind, heart and soul from receiving any word that is contrary to the Word of God. Truthful gossip is still just that—gossip!

Judge everything against the Word of God! Every preacher, teacher, author, television evangelist, missionary—everything you hear and everything you read. The Word of God must be the standard that you compare everything against. This is why it is so important to know the Word of God. You must be able to protect yourself and your family from the many false prophets and teachings that are in the world today.

Finally, what you put in is what comes out. Feed your mind godly principles, and they will come out in your thoughts, words and actions. Feed your mind worldly, fleshly principles and sinful thoughts, and words and actions will follow. James 3:8 says, "But no man can tame the tongue. It is an unruly evil, full of deadly poison." Man cannot tame the tongue but God can through His Word.

**Learn the Word, Love the Word, Live the Word!**

God bless you richly as you study His word and study to show yourself approved unto God.

"Heaven and earth shall pass away but my words shall not pass away" (Matthew. 24:35).

# Birds Of A Feather Flock Together

*1 John 1:7*
*"But if we walk in the light, as he is in the light, we have fellowship one with another, and the blood of Jesus Christ his Son cleanseth us from all sin."*

My wife and I love to go walking at a local park. Sometimes my sister Cathy will go with us for a little exercise as well. This park has beautiful lakes, old style bridges, large green fields where children are playing, people exercising or flying kites and model airplanes, couples having picnics, and families just spending time together. There are also gorgeous ducks and geese swimming in the lakes.

We sat by the lake one day waiting for a friend to come walk with us and I noticed something rather interesting. Whether swimming or on the side of the lake, the ducks huddled with ducks and the geese congregated with geese. Simply put, they were attracted to their own kind. We as the children of God should be attracted to others who have the light of Christ shining in their lives as well. We should be walking in the light as Christ did and that light is what separates us from the world. We are called to be a separate people, holy and set apart from the world and unto Christ. People of light should not take pleasure associating with those in darkness. I'm not referring to witnessing but gather together for the purpose of fellowship and activities.

As we were about to leave, I noticed something quite strange. One lone goose had decided to swim with about ten ducks. It was an awkward site. I noticed the ducks ignored the goose and the other geese ignored the one goose with the wrong crowd. If we as Christians choose to associate with the world, we will eventually find out they do not accept us; and the children of Light cannot accept someone choosing to live in sin. We would be isolated from all, forsaking Christ for a moment of pleasure and ruining our witness in the process! Know who you are, and remember to remain equally yoked with the children of Light rather than a world of darkness.

# Your Worst Enemy: The Word "I"

*Galatians 6:14*
*"But God forbid that I should glory, save in the cross of our Lord Jesus Christ, by whom the world is crucified unto me, and I unto the world."*

How many times do you use the word *I*? It is human nature to desire to boast of our accomplishments and to let others know how wonderful we are. We tend to build ourselves up on our resumes, in job interviews, when we go on first dates, in biographies, etc. We proclaim, "If I don't praise me, who will?"

Paul was writing to the Galatians when he stated in chapter 6, verse 11, "See with what large letters I have written to you with my own hand?" In other words, look what I have done in the flesh! He was stating this not as a matter of pride in himself, but as a way to get his point across to his audience. There were those in the Church who were boasting of their fleshly accomplishments and, in particular, following the law of being circumcised. Paul also stated that, "although these have been circumcised they still do not keep the law."

Boasting of your own accomplishments will never get God's attention! "Look at the church I built!" "Look at all the money I give to missions!" "Look at all the people I feed every month!" These are all wonderful accomplishments; however, Paul in this verse gives us the key to opening the ears and heart of God: We must boast only in the cross of our Lord Jesus Christ by which the world has been crucified. The only act we can boast in is what Christ did for us on the cross. Thank You, Lord Jesus!! Through the cross we have overcome the world and we are dead to the attractions of this world. "Greater is He that is in me than he that is in the world." Whatever you accomplish in this life, be sure to give God all the glory, honor and praise.

# The Beginning And The End

*John 3:16*
*"For God so loved the world, that he gave his only begotten Son, that whosoever believeth in him should not perish, but have everlasting life."*

Remember, the Children of Israel were made to wander in the wilderness for forty years due to their unbelief. However, while in the wilderness, God provided for all of their needs on a daily basis. Fresh water, food, clothing, everything needed to sustain life.

But once again the Children of Israel began to complain and rebelled against Moses and God. (Numbers 21:4-9) They complained about the food, they were tired of wandering in the wilderness, and they were not willing to learn the lessons God wanted them to learn by putting them there in the first place. Due to their complaining and rebelliousness God sent fiery serpents to bite them and kill them. I believe that we can see that God does not appreciate nor tolerate our complaining for very long! Many people died and they went to Moses repenting and wanted God to remove the snakes from their midst.

Then Moses sought the Lord on behalf of the children of Israel and God told him to put a serpent on a stick and lift it up to the wilderness so the people might look upon it and be saved. Once the people looked upon the serpent their bites were healed.

From the very beginning, when Adam and Eve were placed in the Garden of Eden, God's created beings have been rejecting the love and leadership of God. The bible says that Satan rejected God, one third of the angels rejected God with him, and God's finest creation man rejected God. Sin abounded and man lost fellowship with God. But God is slow to anger and longed for man to be restored. So much that He sent His only Son Jesus to redeem mankind. God and Jesus made the ultimate sacrifice and He simply asks us to believe in His son Jesus Christ and to follow Him. If we do so, we will gain eternal life.

As Christ died on the cross he yelled. *"It is finished!"* The ultimate plan of redemption had come to fruition. Jesus became the ultimate living sacrifice, the perfect lamb delivered unto death for mankind. Jesus went to the cross and died to defeat Satan, sin, and the flesh all in one decisive blow. Scripture declares that the serpent would bruise his heel, but He would crush his (Satan's) head (Genesis 3:15). Take a moment right now and praise God for his son Jesus, the victory, and salvation we have through the cross!

Because God so loved—so loved!—the world He gave His only Son. This was the end of sin holding us captive and the beginning of our life living under the shed blood of Jesus! Praise God forevermore. Amen!

# The Law Condemns, Christ Saves

*John 3:17*
*"For God sent not his Son into the world to condemn the world; but that the world through him might be saved."*

"I find you guilty!" declared the Judge. "Officer, take the man away to be put to death!" The law requires justice. The law requires payment. A price must be paid when breaking the law. The worst violations require the ultimate penalty—death.

I was able to walk the tight corridors of a death row unit in a maximum security prison in Texas. I saw the electric chair where inmates were put to death for their transgressions. I spoke with the prison warden and asked him what it felt like to put a man in that chair to die. He replied, "The law mandates death for the crime committed. I cannot stop what is required by law."

The Law of Moses, the Ten Commandments of God, requires us to obey all the law, all the time, to the letter of the law. The problem is we were born into sin, and there is no way that we can meet the standard required by the letter of the law. When Christ came, He expounded on the laws of Moses and stated not only are we required to fulfill the letter of the law but the spirit of the law as well! What!? Who can fulfill such a mandate? Who has not committed one sin of the flesh or of the mind? No one but Christ!

As the above verse states, Christ did not come to condemn the world but to save it by living the only sinless life, therefore fulfilling *ALL* requirements of the law, and then becoming that ultimate "sacrificial lamb" upon Calvary.

The law condemned us but Christ delivered us from that law. Do you truly realize that we are all condemned to die and go to hell because of our guilty status before God, the Almighty Judge? God says, "I find you guilty! Take him from my presence!" Our advocate Jesus says, "Father, I died for his sin, he lives in me, therefore I have already paid the judgment of death on his behalf. You must set him free." God then will accept you without blemish, spot, or wrinkle because you have been washed by the blood of the lamb.

# Bring It On!

*2 Corinthians 12:10*
*"Therefore I take pleasure in infirmities, in reproaches, in necessities, in persecutions, in distresses for Christ's sake: for when I am weak, then am I strong."*

Paul had asked Christ to remove this unknown infirmity from him. But Christ's answer was, "my grace is sufficient for you." Paul stated that he would rather keep his infirmity to ensure that the power of God remained on his life. In this verse he takes it even further. Not only does Paul accept this "thorn in the flesh," he says *bring it on* to anything that tries to come against him. Paul stated that he took pleasure—that means delight, enjoyment, something you want to happen again to you—in many forms of heartaches and infirmities? Bring it on! Reproach? Bring it on! Persecution? Bring it on! Distress? Bring it on! Bring it all on for Christ's sake. In other words, I will go through anything this world has to throw at me so I may glorify Jesus! With each beating, shipwreck, imprisonment, flogging, Paul says, "Is that all you've got? I will take this and much more so that one person might come to know Christ."

How about you? Are you a Christian when it is convenient? When it is safe and acceptable? How much have you suffered for Christ? How much are you willing to suffer for His name sake? Or will you say as Paul in this verse, "For when I am weak, then I am strong." Because having less of self means having more of Christ in your life. Get rid of the flesh, the sin, the stubbornness, the pride, and the arrogance, and turn your life completely over the Lord. Then you too can say to this world, "Bring it on!"

# God's Grace Is Enough

*2 Corinthians 12:9*
*"And he said unto me, My grace is sufficient for thee: for my strength is made perfect in weakness. Most gladly therefore will I rather glory in my infirmities, that the power of Christ may rest upon me."*

Paul had been given a thorn in the flesh by the Lord. He had asked three times for it to be removed but God decided not to honor the prayer. God said to Paul, "My grace is sufficient for you." Paul had been given many visions, had been used mightily of God and could have felt privileged above others. God's answer says that God will give the miraculous, but he also wants to keep us grounded. A thorn in Paul's flesh was given to ensure he maintained being humble.

Paul said the love of God passes all of our knowledge and our ability to comprehend. It's beyond our grasp in these dusty containers we currently call home. But we would have to understand, comprehend, and digest the love of God to be filled with all the fullness of God!

The same God that we cannot fully comprehend or understand—that fullness of God—lives in us! Paul is telling us to comprehend God, experience God, and be *filled* with God. Then (and this verse overwhelms me) Paul is saying "to Him (God) who is able to do exceedingly abundantly above all that we *ask* or *think*, according to the power that works in us, to Him be glory!"

The God of love, the "I sent my perfect, holy Son for a rebellious race" kind of love, who wants us to comprehend the fullness of that love is able to do more than I can ask or think. And it is all according to the power of God that works in us! We may seek for God to use us in mighty ways but realize there is a price to pay. God may use you to heal others but you may never receive healing. Others may be blessed mightily by your ministry and you can barely pay the bills. Others get promoted and you still have to deal with the crooked boss who condemns your every decision.

Whatever the case, God's answer is, "My grace is enough for you." Paul makes it very clear that he would rather boast in his infirmities and have the power of God in his life. Can you say the same thing for your life?

# The Mystery Of God

*Ephesians 3:20*
*"Now unto him that is able to do exceeding abundantly above all that we ask or think, according to the power that worketh in us."*

"Yes, Jesus loves me, the bible tells me so." So simple, we teach it to our youngest children. Yet, this song may hold reference to the mystery of God. Leading up to this scripture, Paul is trying to help us understand and appreciate the great mystery of God's love.

Paul is asking God to strengthen our inner man with His Spirit that we may be able to fully comprehend this mystery. Christ must dwell in our hearts through faith, and we must be rooted and grounded in His love.

The love of God! Paul wants us to catch a glimpse of how big the love of God is. How wide is God's love? How long? How deep and how tall? We cannot fully know the answer to these questions in our present state. Think of the east from the west, up from down, and that is the beginning of our Father's love for us. According to the power that works in us, our God can do more than we can ask or think—and that power is in you, in me at all times!

But here is the amazing thing. Paul mentions all of this as an afterthought. The focus is on love and is not on what He can do. Paul is telling us to passionately praise our God! Passionately worship the God who loves without end and dwells in our hearts. There is not enough knowledge in this world to understand his fullness, and the thought that He can do more than we have ever imagined—worship Him! Worship Him! Worship Him! What foolish creatures we are to doubt that God can solve any problem we may have. Thank you Lord for your love and mercy upon sinful man!

# Write The Vision

*Habakkuk 2:2*
*"And the Lord answered me, and said, Write the vision, and make it plain upon tables, that he may run that readeth it."*

God wants you to seek Him for direction in life. He wants you to trust Him and pray that God will give you a vision of purpose for your life, your family, your church, your city, and even our nation. Seek God, hear from the Lord, and then He says to "write the vision, make it plain in tablets, so He may run who reads it."

What is God calling you to do? Once you know, write it down and put it where you can see it every day, make it easy to understand, and then, go for it! Is it a vision for your family, where you want them to go, and become in the Lord? Write it down and give it to every family member to see everyday! Print it, post it in a prominent place for all to see. Catch the vision and run with it. The vision should be encouraging, uplifting, challenging, and most importantly, God ordained. Take your faith to a new level and develop a vision that only God could accomplish! "Greater is He that is in me than He that is in the world" (1 John 4:4).

Seek a vision, write it down, run with it, and believe it will happen in Jesus' name!

# Lord, How Long?

*Habukkuk 2:3*
*"For the vision is yet for an appointed time, but at the end it shall speak, and not lie: though it tarry, wait for it; because it will surely come, it will not tarry."*

The vision is received, written, you're running with it, but you see no results. Now "faith is the substance of things hoped for and the evidence of things not seen" (Hebrews 11:1).

Don't stop now! Believe God is working a mighty miracle through your God-given vision. Pray, seek God, read His word, and **BELIEVE** God is moving on your behalf. When I was pastoring I set a vision for the entire church. I posted it, got the people excited about it, preached the mighty things God was about to do through the vision, and—nothing! Lord, did I hear you correctly? Are You in this vision or was it just me? He answered softly but with power, "I am the giver but I have work to do in you and in the church before you are ready for the vision to be accomplished."

Keep your faith in God. Prepare yourself to receive the vision into your life. The vision is for an appointed time. A time appointed set by God Himself! But this verse also says that "at the end it will speak and it will not lie." The vision will come to pass if you prepare for it, tarry for it, pray and have faith for it, and be ready to receive the vision into your life. It will be a living testimony to the world that God is moving mightily in your life. Be sure to give God all the glory for giving the vision and completing it in you at the appointed time.

# Mayday! Mayday!

*Matthew 5:16*
*"Let your light so shine before men, that they may see your good works, and glorify your Father which is in heaven."*

A large storm is pounding away at a ship in the sea. It's dark, the storm is climaxing, and the waves are tossing the ship like a leaf in the wind. The captain knows that he is close to shore and is afraid of crashing against the rocks and sinking his vessel with everyone on board. "Where is that lighthouse? I am lost at sea without it!" The Captain calls on the radio, "Mayday! Mayday!" Suddenly, and not a moment too soon, the captain sees the bright beam of light from the Lighthouse! It's not just light but it is hope, salvation, and the lifeline that was desperately needed to avoid disaster. He has his bearing and knows which direction to go. He knows whose he is! He is able to avoid disaster all because of the saving power of the light.

The darker the night, the more the light shines. We live in a dark and perverted world. It is being tossed to and fro by the power of sin and transgression. There is only one Light of hope and that is in the saving power of Jesus shining forth in your life!

Matthew says that we are the light of the world. We must shine forth strongly and proclaim Jesus as Lord so the world will not crash against the rocky shore and go to hell. A light that is shining brightly cannot be hidden. Darkness cannot be where there is light.

Your good works are as a shining light to this dark world. When you love as Jesus loved, they will see the light. When you serve as Jesus served, they see the light.

When you praise God in the midst of the storm, your light burns brighter. When you count all trials and tribulations as joy your light burns brilliantly. The world will hate you as they hated Christ. However, when you still show them love and forgiveness your light will be the light of salvation and a ray of hope in a horrible storm! Let your light so shine so that man may glorify your Father in heaven.

# Follow The Money

*Matthew 6:21*
*"For where your treasure is, there will your heart be also."*

I saw a gospel tract many years ago entitled, "He with the most toys wins." The tract was stating that many times in life we want more and more, then a little more.

If you want to know what is important to a person, just follow the money. People will invest in what they truly desire and want. Where are you investing your money? For years, I would have answered with the idol of sports. Golf was a major expense for me. Hey, I deserved it. I worked hard and I needed to rest, relax, and have quality "me" time. I always needed (well, wanted) the newest and best golf related items. There were new clubs, new waterproof cleatless shoes, golf clothing that didn't look like it came straight from the 70s, balls that were guaranteed to go straight (sure), personalized tees, and that elusive club membership. The majority of my unspecified funds were going to pleasing myself.

I finally realized that golf had become my idol. I worshipped it and put my money into my first love. I knew that God was asking me to invest in His kingdom more than into my earthly pleasures.

What do you love the most? A simple way to find out is to follow your money. Are you investing in the things of God such as His church, missions, blessing others that are less fortunate, and the furtherance of the Gospel of Christ? Or are the things of this world such as sports, amusements, worldly pleasures, houses, bigger cars, the latest electronic gadget, or possibly a hidden pleasure taking your heart from God? You can be assured God knows where your heart is and He will bless you according to your faithfulness to Him and His kingdom. Seek heavenly treasures and you cannot lose!

# 100 Years Versus Eternity

*Matthew 16:26*
*"For what is a man profited, if he shall gain the whole world, and lose his own soul? or what shall a man give in exchange for his soul?"*

One hundred years or eternity? Which amount of time would you rather have everything that you ever wanted plus so much more?

In the verses right before this one, Christ states that a man must deny himself, take up his cross, and follow Him. He also says to save your life you must lose it, but if you lose your life for Him you will find it. Confusing? Simply stated, while you're on this earth 70, 80, or even 100 years, you must deny yourself and follow Him to win. First of all, you get to avoid all of the trappings of this sin filled world. Christ is looking for those individuals who will put His will first in their lives. Secondly, by denying self you get to partake in all of the blessings of the Lord during your time here on earth AND for eternity. Now I'm not a genius but to deny the desires of the flesh and the world for up to 100 years to get salvation and to be in His presence for eternity seems like a bargain.

He never promised that it would be easy. He simply wants us to accept Him, pick up His cross, which is His gospel and tell everyone that we can. We can expect to receive what He received from the world: hatred, resentment, anger, rejection, hostility, and possibly even death. In fact, if you are not seeing these things manifested towards you from the world, there is a major problem with your witness. But it is all temporal, all just for a season. Once this life is over, you will begin your eternal life in the presence of God forever! You will receive rewards based on your service while here on earth. Better to plant for a season so we may reap the harvest for the rest of our life!

You do the math!

# If – What A Difference It Makes!

*2 Chronicles 7:14*
*"If my people, which are called by my name, shall humble themselves, and pray, and seek my face, and turn from their wicked ways; then will I hear from heaven, and will forgive their sin, and will heal their land."*

I could fly—*If* I had wings.

"If" is a small word but makes a major difference on the subject. The statement, "I can fly" must be explained by "if I had wings." That is the condition nature has set forth to have the ability to fly. There is no way around the fact. No wishing, willing, desiring or any other feeling will produce flying. We can build machines with wings but for a person to literally fly they would have to have wings, at least if they want to fly more than one time!

Our country is being judged by God. Actually, we have condemned ourselves due to our actions. We have turned our backs on God. This country was founded on godly principles such as, "In God We Trust," prayer, seeking God for direction and guidance, blessing others, and obeying His laws. America has banned prayer, we do not seek or want His leadership and guidance, and our country murders millions of babies every year in the name of choice. Our leaders intentionally avoid mentioning the name of God in public, the Ten Commandments have been outlawed for public display, gay marriage and other sins are promoted as civil rights. No wonder God is forced to judge such an evil and godless society. He judged Sodom. He judged the kingdom of Israel and the kingdom of Judah because they rejected Him and served "other gods."

However, God loves us so much He gives us an "if." *If* my people, which are called by my name. . . God still loves us! He still claims us. He says, "You're mine and you have my name. *If* you will humble yourselves."

There must be humility before revival. There must be a contrite spirit before God is able to move on our behalf. Set aside the arrogance and believing you are right before God. Humble yourself and pray, seek His face. Call upon the name of the Lord! Seek and you will find the favor of God. "The effectual, fervent prayer of a righteous man availeth much" (James 5:16).

But there is more you must do and that is turn from your wicked ways. Repent, go in the opposite direction. Turn from sin unto the Lord as fast as you can and you can be saved. *If* you are humble, pray, seek His face, turn from your wickedness, *then* God will hear you, forgive you, and heal the land.

There is still hope for America! But we need men and women of God to stand up for righteousness and proclaim it to everyone who will listen. Remember, we as a nation have brought this judgment to our nation ourselves. God is a just God, and although He loves us, He must punish sin. Pray right now that God will save our country from pending destruction!

# Pray Without Ceasing

*1 Thessalonians 5:17*
*"Pray without ceasing."*

Do you remember the day you started dating someone you really liked? You would call them a dozen times a day, talk constantly on the phone, even hours at a time? Many of us remember when there were no computers, Facebook, emails, Twitter, or Skype. There was just "Ma Bell" telephone service or visiting in person! Remember how you just loved seeing that individual, and when you left you could not wait to be with her/him again? Why? Because you longed to get to know her/him better, to know her/his thoughts and desires.

I remember when my wife and I were dating. I could not get enough of her! I loved the way she looked, her fragrance, the twinkle in her eyes when she looked at me. I realized the more I got to know her the more I wanted to know! She was and still is an amazing woman that God has blessed me with as a helper.

The Word of God commands us to pray without ceasing. Prayer is just communication with our heavenly Father. We should desire Him and His fellowship so much more than any person in our life. We should desire to spend time with Him more than any person. God says know me, seek me, test me, desire me, love me, worship me and I will make myself known to you. We can know as much of God as we are willing to pursue.

The scripture says to pray without ceasing. This means speak to the Lord continually. He is the friend who is always with you and can guide you through every situation. We are to be in an attitude of prayer throughout the day. Quote His scriptures to receive encouragement or to defeat temptation that comes your way and to minister to others. If you love Him you will seek Him and will want to communicate with Him every moment of the day.

# Pass The Salt?

Matthew 5:13
*"Ye are the salt of the earth: but if the salt have lost his savor, wherewith shall it be salted? it is thenceforth good for nothing, but to be cast out, and to be trodden under foot of men."*

"Aren't you going to taste that first?" I hear that from my wife as I am adding salt to my meal every so often. I have become so used to food needing salt that I occasionally do not taste it before adding salt to be sure. My wife and my doctor have both informed me that I need to watch my salt intake.

Salt is a wonderful thing. There are many uses for salt. If you pack meat in salt it will preserve the taste and will prevent the meat from rotting. Salt will also clean many stains when applied properly. Salt can make something that is drab and bland taste flavorful and enjoyable. Seasoning is important.

God says that we are to be salt of the world. We are to be the flavor of God in the dull world. We should be the salt that adds flavor and brings people to the saving message of Jesus Christ.

But for salt to be effective in any way it must come in contact with something. You can praise salt and look at it in its container and say how wonderful salt would taste, but it will be of no benefit if it never comes in contact with food. We as Christians must also come in contact with the world to provide the flavor of God to them. The world will savor the wonderful taste of our Lord Jesus Christ and crave to know Him.

"Babydoll, dinner looks great! Where's the salt?"

# Where's The Finish Line?

*Galatians 6:9*
*"And let us not be weary in well doing: for in due season we shall reap, if we faint not."*

In 2011 I made the decision to run in a half-marathon. So I tell my wife that *we* are going to train for a half-marathon and she replied, "Really? Let's do it!" I don't know if I was hoping she would say, no way! Or, that's crazy! But once she said yes, I was committed.

We ran every day according to our training schedule. There were days we did not feel well, we were tired, or we just did not really want to be committed to the race. But we were diligent and faithful to our training runs (most of the time). We ran on hot day, rainy days, we ran in the darkness of the night and even when others wanted us to make plans. To be honest, there were some days that we felt so bad that we did not run. Some days it was hard to keep my eyes on the race and the reward of finishing the half-marathon. But when I failed to train I got right back to it the next day. My wife was like that energizer bunny — she just kept going and going and going. She was a great training partner and kept me motivated when I couldn't find strength myself.

I learned some things that really helped me in my training. I registered for the race early. I really felt invested and committed when I did that! I had spent the money and marked it on my calendar so it was a definite go. Also I began to tell people that I was running a half-marathon so they would always ask me how my training was going. I met others who were training as well for the half-marathon and we would encourage one another. We would talk about the type of shoes we wore and the places we trained and our running strategies. I had run the race a hundred times in my mind and I knew I was going to start and finish the race!

On race day my wife and I were very excited and nervous. We arrived early, stretched, and began to look at everyone else who was there. There were thousands of people all decked out in their running outfits. They had on tights, compression socks, alien looking sunglasses, ear buds, and sweat-repelling shirts with all types of logos on them. We had on tee shirts and basic running shorts.

We lined up for the start. The gun went off and we took off running our race. I felt really good. The adrenaline carried me the first three or four miles with no problem. I began to feel the burn around mile eight but kept a pretty good pace. However, around mile ten I was saying (actually whispering due to breathing so hard) where is the finish line? I was tired, hurting, felt defeated and all alone. No one had warned me about the effects of chaffing, wearing the proper socks, or the purpose of wearing tights (I was learning very quickly). But as I prayed and asked God for strength I remembered this verse: "Do not grow weary! We shall reap if we faint not." I found the energy to continue, not at the fastest pace but continue nonetheless. When I got to mile thirteen I knew someone had to be playing a cruel joke on me. I had already run at least twenty miles it seemed and the finish line kept moving away from me! But then I caught a glimpse of it. I regained my desire and vision of the finish line to run towards it. As I entered the stadium to cross the finish line I heard the songs playing, the crowd cheering, and realized they were cheering for me! As I crossed the finish line, Mayor Strange of Montgomery was there to congratulate me! I had run my race and finished. I was number 932! I stayed at the finish line until my wife appeared and was able to cheer for her as she finished her race. It was an extremely emotional and glorious moment to be able to celebrate such an accomplishment with my wife!

Our Christian faith is the same as the half-marathon. Do not grow weary in doing well. Live for Christ! There will be trouble (like chaffing), tribulation, exhaustion, and even the desire to give up at times. But trust in God, call upon His name, and He will give you the strength you need to overcome every temptation, mountain, and road block in your life.

The finish line is very close! Jesus will be coming for His bride very soon and we must not grow weary in watching and waiting for Him. In due season, we will reap a wonderful harvest for serving Him—if we do not faint or fall away. Remember, Jesus Christ has already finished His race and will be there to welcome us across the finish line with the words, "Well done thy good and faithful servant! Enter thou into the joy of the Lord!"

# I Feel Like A New Man

*2 Corinthians 5:17*
*"Therefore if any man be in Christ, he is a new creature: old things are passed away; behold, all things are become new."*

"Okay. It's you and me. One of us is going down! I will fight you to the very end!" What am I talking about? I'm referring to what I say to my yard on the weekends! The grass and weeds to cut, bushes to trim, the pine straw to collect, the kudzu to cut back, poison ivy to defeat, the debris to clear from the lawn, etc. It's a battle to be won or lost! I do all the things necessary to defeat the evil empire of the lawn every week and it fights back.

I prepare my weapons of war such as the lawn mower, the weed eater, the clippers, the leaf blower, and the all important gloves. I hear the theme of the *Good, the Bad and the Ugly* in my head as I stare down the evil empire of grass, pollen and poison ivy. I take the offensive and work hard engaging the bushes, limbs and kudzu, known to many down south as the weed of the devil! I get sweaty as I cut the grass. The yard strikes back at me covering me in dirt, dust and pollen. The poison ivy lashes out and attempts to cover me with its poisonous leaves and moisture. By the time I am through with this battle I emerge victorious but not unscathed. I am covered from head to toe, and my nose and eyes are running from all of the dust and pollen. I am feeling tired, drained, and sore from the mighty battle. As I head back into the garage to put away my weapons of battle, the lawn trolls yell at me, "We will be back stronger and taller next week!"

When I head into the house to take a rest, my wife says, "What happened to you? You look horrible! Don't sit on anything! Go take a shower." But Babydoll, I'm tired and barely won the victory today. I need to rest. So as I head to the shower. . . (you see who had the last word).

I shower and allow the refreshing water to cover me. It takes all of the dirt, dust, pollen filth and sweat and washes it all away. I begin to feel renewed and refreshed. I just soak in the waterfall of water and allow it to rejuvenate me. I put on clean clothes and go into the kitchen where I declare to my wife, "I feel like a new man!" It's amazing what a little soap and water can do for you.

How much more do we need to be cleansed from the dirt, filth, and sin of this world? The old nature is very sinful and carnal. But when we accept Jesus Christ as our Lord and Savior, we become new creatures. The blood of Christ washes away all of our sin and filth and God is able to look upon us as His holy people. Just like after the shower I felt like a new man. Once you're in Christ old things are passed away. They are never to be found again just like the dirt and grime washed away by the water, going down the drain to never be seen again. People should see a difference in your life. You should think differently, you should act differently and treat people differently. You're still in the world but a new creature, a living sacrifice for Jesus! You will still have the battles to fight. You will still be attacked by sinful thoughts and the lusts of this world. But you already have the victory. You know it and the devil knows it. So go forth and fight knowing you will come out victoriously.

Every day I see the yard and it reminds me of the battle to come. But I'm ready, prepared, and have the strength needed to defeat it.

By the way, I'd better sharpen those lawnmower blades. . .

# Do You Have An Inner Circle?

James 5:16
"Confess your faults one to another, and pray one for another, that ye may be healed. The effectual fervent prayer of a righteous man availeth much."

When people in the church need prayer or counseling, they usually go to the pastor. Where does the pastor go when he needs to vent, confess, and ask for prayer? Sadly, too many pastors have no one and they try to make it through their life and ministry alone.

My brother Robert has a unique ministry called Barnabas Counseling. He ministers to pastors, clergy, and churches when they are hurting. He also provides mediation when churches are in times of disagreement. He has filled a void so that many pastors can have someone to talk with or pray with. When the fellowship through which he is ordained has a pastor experiencing a moral failure, they send the pastor and his family to my brother for counseling. He is the minister to the minister. Many lives and churches have been saved because of the Lord working through his ministry. (His website is barnabascounseling.org if you know of any church or minister who is in need of someone to encourage and guide them through a difficult situation.)

It is very important for everyone to have prayer partners. This is an inner circle of individuals whom you can trust with your life. These are individuals with whom you can share your doubts, fears and sins, and they do not judge you; they support you, encourage you, and pray with and for you. When choosing these individuals you need to ensure they are righteous before the Lord. People who love you enough to be honest with you, yet tarry before the Lord and call down heaven on your behalf. It is always wise when choosing your prayer partners that men have men partners and women should have women partners. There are times when you are going to spend quality time together praying, sharing about your desires and struggles and tarrying before the Lord. You do not want to give the devil any area to use against you. Especially, when your inner circle should be the closest people to you in the entire world.

This scripture calls for us to confess our faults to each other, and pray for each other that we may be healed. Healing comes in many forms such as physical, spiritual and emotional. But God calls for the prayers of a righteous individual who offers effective, fervent prayers. God will answer this type of prayer because you are seeking the face of God in the right manner.

I am a member of my brother's inner circle and I pray for him every day. I know that God is using him in a mighty way and I'm blessed to be a part of his ministry.

# Daddy, Please!

*Matthew 7:7*
*"Ask, and it shall be given you; seek, and ye shall find; knock, and it shall be opened unto you:"*

I have a beautiful daughter named Carissa Danielle whom God has blessed me with for the past 20 years. I know most men want a son but I prayed and asked my Heavenly Father for a beautiful daughter and he honored my request. Carissa has always been a "daddy's girl." She definitely knows how to pull my heartstrings! Throughout the years she has asked for things, and I do my best to give her what she wants. As a father, I want her to have good things, to be blessed, and to be prepared for this life. There were times she would ask for items that were not good for her and I had to say no. It was my job to protect her, love her, and help her mature as she got older. As much as she asked for things, I would buy her gifts when she did not ask just because I loved her and wanted to bless her.

Our Heavenly Father will do so much more for us than we can as earthly fathers. He loves us and will give us what this passage says. As much as I wanted to care for and give good things to my daughter because I love her, our Heavenly Father will do so much more for us! God is waiting in heaven for us to ask so he can give; seek Him so He can give us the answers and knock so He can open the right doors for our journey. Trust God for all things in your life because He never gets tired of us asking, seeking, and knocking.

I am so proud of the godly woman my daughter has become. We should want our Heavenly Father to say the same about us as well.

# Garbage In, Garbage Out

*Philippians 4:8*
*"Finally, brethren, whatsoever things are true, whatsoever things are honest, whatsoever things are just, whatsoever things are pure, whatsoever things are lovely, whatsoever things are of good report; if there be any virtue, and if there be any praise, think on these things."*

Put enough garbage together and it will begin to stink! Garbage smells bad enough, but let it sit in the heat for a while and it is unbearable! The true stench begins to come out. Not only does garbage stink, it also makes the containers it is in stink as well. The garbage has to be emptied then the container must be washed as well to get rid of the remnants the garbage left behind.

Have you become a garbage dump for others? Do you allow others to dump things into your life that are not pleasing to God? Strife, gossip (yes, gossip is gossip even if it is true), rumors about others, discouraging words, negativity, criticism, back-biting, slander, etc. All of these things are garbage in the eyes of God and will eventually make you stink! If you allow these items to be deposited into your life, then you will eventually begin letting them out through your own lips. If you are feeding your mind with garbage, then out comes garbage through your words, actions, and attitudes.

Paul is encouraging us to guard our attitudes and minds by thinking on positive, godly traits — things that are true, noble (honorable), just, pure, lovely, good report, virtue, praiseworthy. Think on these things. Meditate on these wonderful items. If you do, your attitude, thoughts and actions will reflect what you are putting into your mind and heart.

It's your choice — stink like a garbage bin, or be a fragrant pleasing smell unto God.

# Don't Worry, Be Happy

*Philippians 4:6*
*"Be careful for nothing; but in every thing by prayer and supplication with thanksgiving let your requests be made known unto God."*

There was a popular song many years ago by the title of "Don't Worry, Be Happy." It was a catchy little tune with a simple message—don't worry and be happy. That was it! It had an up-tempo, Jamaican beat that made people feel good.

Many people have a hard time not worrying about the issues of their lives. Statistics show that up to 90% of the fears that people worry about never occur. That is a lot of time wasted worrying about things that never even happen. It has also been proven that worry causes stress and can actually cause long-term diseases within the body. The mind is a powerful tool and your thoughts and your attitudes can effect, alter, and even cause physical ailments.

A Christian should be the last group of people to worry. We have an open line to our heavenly Father every second of every day! We do not need to worry but take everything in prayer to the Lord.

Paul is asking us "why worry about anything?" But in all things pray, put all of the facts on the table before the Lord, and let your requests be made known with thanksgiving. Don't forget the past. Many times we go before the Lord begging Him to change our circumstances, but we do not take the time to thank Him for everything He has already done for us. Has the Lord ever met your needs? Hasn't He proven His faithfulness to you many times over? Why do we have such short memories when it comes to the blessings of God and how He has delivered us out of the hands of our enemy time and time again?

You have a need? Don't worry—go to God in prayer! This is an attitude adjustment. Instead of spending time worrying, being anxious, and fretting, turn everything over to the Lord in prayer. Thank God for providing you with the answer even before it has arrived.

Worry equals not trusting the Lord to provide for all of your needs. You need to learn to not be anxious; take it all to God in prayer. He will guard your heart and mind. He will see your faithfulness and reward you with the perfect answer. We are God's children and He will certainly provide for our every need and in every situation. If you put your needs in the Lord's hands, you can be assured you will receive the best possible answer—and your life will be much more peaceful as well.

You'll also feel much better!

# What Do I Say?

*Romans 8:26*
*"Likewise the Spirit also helpeth our infirmities: for we know not what we should pray for as we ought: but the Spirit itself maketh intercession for us with groanings which cannot be uttered."*

I had to preach the funeral of a young man from our church. He was only 16 years old but loved the Lord mightily. He was active in church, a strong witness before his friends, a great athlete, and a loving son. He had proclaimed to the congregation just a month earlier that he wanted to serve the Lord in full-time ministry. His parents could not have been prouder of him. Then it happened.

One night after a football game he was driving home and was hit by a drunk driver. He only had a few miles to go before reaching home. Many of his classmates passed the wreck praying for whoever was involved but not knowing it was one of their own. The state trooper who came to his parents' home said he was killed instantly. The man who hit him was drunk and did not get hurt at all. It was a horrible time for everyone close to this family.

The father and mother wanted to say a few words at the funeral but as they stood there over their son's casket, the words would not come out. They both began to cry and mourn before the Lord. A time that seemed to last for hours was actually only a few moments. I went and stood by those parents, comforted them, and led them to their seats. I knew I would have to speak for them.

Have you ever hurt so much you could not speak? Have you been at a loss of words and even if you could speak you would not know what to say? Even in prayer? This is when the Holy Spirit, who resides inside of you, will pray for you unto the Lord. We may not know the words to pray or even what to ask for, but the Holy Spirit knows every time! He will intercede for us to the King of Kings and the Lord of Lords. The sounds you make while the Spirit is praying may sound like groaning or mourning, but God knows exactly what is being said. This type of prayer takes you to the next level. Who else is better equipped to intercede on your behalf than the Holy Spirit? He is God and He knows what to say. He lives in us, so He knows our needs and represents us better than we could ourselves.

In fact, you should pray in the Spirit every time you pray. When you feel inadequate in your prayer life, when you feel you're not getting your prayers past the ceiling of the room you are in, let the Holy Spirit take control and ramp up your prayers. The Holy Spirit will never let you down!

# Are You Resisting Or Inviting?

*James 4:7*
*"Submit yourselves therefore to God. Resist the devil, and he will flee from you."*

Submission is a hard thing to do. To submit means to make yourself vulnerable and to trust the one you are submitting before. We have a very smart four year-old standard poodle named Sadie. She is very loving and enjoys being in our presence all the time. To show that she has submitted to us as her masters, she will lay on her back with her belly showing. This is a sign of submission. She is very vulnerable in this position. She does this because she knows we will not harm her. She also loves to have her tummy rubbed! I believe she knows we will protect her from any harm that comes her way.

God says to submit ourselves to Him. We must humbly come before the Lord and give ourselves completely to Him. We must lay prostrate before the Lord and tell Him we surrender all of ourselves to Him. Once we submit unto God, the scripture declares if we resist the devil he will flee. Submitting before God produces humility and humility will chase worldliness from your life.

Many Christians are having trouble with sin in their lives because instead of resisting the devil, they are inviting him into their life! To resist the devil you must fill yourself with God, His Word, think on godly thoughts, and be involved in godly activities. It's hard to sin when you are in an attitude of prayer, worship, or thanksgiving unto our Lord!

Only when we take our eyes and focus off the Lord do we give the devil an opportunity to tempt us. You are more vulnerable to attacks of the devil when you are tired, depressed, discouraged, disillusioned, or angry. When he comes to tempt you, use the Word of God to resist the devil and make him flee. Do not give him a foot in the threshold of your soul.

Remember the old saying, the devil made me do it? He can only *tempt* you to do it, and that is only if you let him into your spiritual house.

Resist the devil and he will flee from you. That's a promise of God's Holy Word!

# Where Is God?

*James 4:8*
*"Draw nigh to God, and he will draw nigh to you. Cleanse your hands, ye sinners; and purify your hearts, ye double minded."*

We previously discussed James 4:7. As children of God, we are to submit to God and resist the devil. If you resist, the devil will flee from you. God wants His people to be humble. God opposes the proud but helps the humble.

Verse 8 takes it one step further. Not only are we to submit to God but we are to draw near to God. If you do not feel God's presence, who do you think has moved away? Not God. He longs for fellowship with His children. If you seek God and draw closer to Him, He will draw near to you. You must make the first step because God is already waiting for you! God will never force Himself upon His people. He proves His love for us over and over, and we continue to reject Him over and over. But He never leaves us. He remains constant; when we disobey and become proud we are the ones walking away from Him.

He says as we draw near to Him we must cleanse our hands. This means do away with works of the flesh. Be finished with our sinful nature and lusts and return to our first love of the Lord.

We must also purify our hearts. We cannot serve two masters. We cannot say that we love God then serve the devil or the flesh with our thoughts and actions. He says that is being double-minded. James also says that a double-minded man is unstable in all of his ways. He is compared to a ship that is tossed side to side by the sea and the wind. James also says a man that prays but lack faith in God is also double-minded.

Submit to God, resist the devil, draw near to God, and clean your hands and heart to be steadfast in the faith and the love of God. Remember, if you can't find God, He is not the one who has moved away!

# Most Enduring Possession

*Isaiah 40:8*
*"The grass withereth, the flower fadeth: but the word of our God shall stand for ever."*

When we look at our possessions we usually buy warranties with them. If they come with a warranty the salesperson will ask, "Do you want an extended warranty to protect your purchase?" Nowadays if an item lasts several years it's amazing. Cars usually last eight to ten years before they start falling apart. Appliances may last that long before needing constant repairs. Houses may last twenty-five to thirty-five years before they need serious repairs.

But there is one possession you have that God says will never change, spoil, need repairs or diminish—His Word! In this verse God says that as the grass withers and the flowers fade, people too have a limited amount of time before they expire. Even though some people in the Old Testament lived much longer than we do today (700-900 years) they too had an expiration date. But the Word of God will stand forever— through the tribulation, the millennium, the new heavens and earth, and into God's eternal kingdom. The words of hope, inspiration, and guidance you read today will be the same one million years from now. Now that's a warranty!

We can be assured that everything guaranteed and promised to us in the Word of God is going to happen. If you want to give someone a gift of a lifetime and beyond, give them the life-changing Word of God!

# The Calling Of God

*1 Peter 2:9*
*"But ye are a chosen generation, a royal priesthood, an holy nation, a peculiar people; that ye should shew forth the praises of him who hath called you out of darkness into his marvelous light."*

Have you been called of God for a purpose? Yes, all believers can state they have been called of God. Peter mentions five times in this book that the believers have a general yet specific call upon their lives to be holy and unto Christ.

*"But as he which hath called you is holy, so be ye holy in all manner of conversation" (1 Peter 1:15).*

*"For even hereunto were ye called: because Christ also suffered for us, leaving us an example, that ye should follow his steps:" 1 Peter 3:9 "Not rendering evil for evil, or railing for railing: but contrariwise blessing; knowing that ye are thereunto called, that ye should inherit a blessing." 1 Peter 5:10 "But the God of all grace, who hath called us unto his eternal glory by Christ Jesus, after that ye have suffered a while, make you perfect, stablish, strengthen, settle you.")*

We could not come to the saving grace of our Lord Jesus Christ without God calling us to His Son. This general calling is offered to everyone. Anyone who responds to Him is considered "the called."

There is also a call that is very specific to an individual. This call is to serve the body of Christ through such positions as elders, teachers, pastors, missionaries, evangelists, etc. This call is witnessed and confirmed by an individual's heart and an outward recognition of the body of Christ.

All of us are a chosen generation, a royal priesthood and a holy nation. A very special people set apart by God for God. Why? So we may proclaim the praises of Him who has called us out of darkness into His marvelous light. If you are a true child of God, set apart by God and for God, you will proclaim His praise to the earth! Are you telling others about the goodness of God? Sharing all of the wonderful blessings He is giving to you and your family? How He saved you from the law of death and gave you eternal life? If not, why not?

Have you ever been in total darkness? I'm talking about so dark you can't see your hand directly in front of your face. God has called you from a place of total darkness into His marvelous light! Praise God! I'll take the light over darkness every time.

Don't be selfish. Tell someone the good news so they may answer the call of God from the darkness of sin into His wonderful, marvelous light from this point until eternity.

# Every Eye Shall Behold Him

*Revelation 1:7*
*"Behold, he cometh with clouds; and every eye shall see him, and they also which pierced him: and all kindreds of the earth shall wail because of him. Even so, Amen."*

The scripture declares that when Christ returns, "every eye shall see Him." How is this possible? Remember this is referring to when Christ comes back with His saints to fight the armies of the world that have gathered against Israel. Before our generation this might not have been possible. But today with television, satellites, and all types of instant media such as the internet, Twitter, and Skype, you can see any event from around the world as it is unfolding! Is this how God is going to do it? I don't know, but the Word of God declares it will happen so it is a fact in my book.

God could cause Christ to appear around the world or gather everyone unto Christ. The important thing is it will happen and the people of the earth will mourn because of Him. He will come to save the city of Jerusalem and the nation of Israel from the wolf nations of the world.

We have two choices: either fear Him when He returns to defeat the world, or be with Him as He returns as the victorious King of Israel.

# Someone's Watching You

*Luke 15:10*
*"Likewise, I say unto you, there is joy in the presence of the angels of God over one sinner that repenteth."*

Once someone passes from this world to heaven, what happens? Hebrews 12:1 states that we are surrounded by a great cloud of witnesses. Are they actually witnesses to what is happening here on earth? This scripture states there is "rejoicing in the presence of angels of God over one sinner who repents." Who is rejoicing over the sinners being saved and how are they aware?

Perhaps the saints who are now in heaven are aware of activities on earth. God rejoices over a sinner accepting His son Jesus, but perhaps all of the saints rejoice as well! They have experienced this conversion and are living proof of the reality of the promises of God. If they can rejoice over this fact then perhaps they can see other activities here and are interceding for their loved ones. Is it possible? God's Word tells us that Christ sits at the right hand of the Father and He is interceding on our behalf.

I won't presume to know for sure, but maybe I have made you think a little bit deeper. If I am right then you have many people who are rooting for you and waiting to see you again at a wonderful day of homecoming. Don't disappoint them!

# A Resurrected Body

*Acts 1:3*
*"To whom also he shewed himself alive after his passion by many infallible proofs, being seen of them forty days, and speaking of the things pertaining to the kingdom of God."*

Christ is alive, raised from the dead. This is a proven fact. This scripture declares that Christ, after dying on the cross, showed himself to a number of people over a forty day period. As Christ did this He was walking on this earth in His glorified, resurrected body. He was not a spirit. He did not leave his earthly body in the grave. He testified to his disciples that "it is I myself" to tell them He was body and spirit.

Thomas was able to feel the nail prints in His hands and feet. They were real. Christ's appearance on this earth in His resurrected body is a testimony that our resurrected bodies will be made to exist on the new earth. It will be a body but new and improved. People will recognize you and you will recognize them.

No matter the make, model or condition of your current body, you will get the newest and best model possible in the new earth.

# Your Eyes Speak For Your Heart

*Colossians 3:1-2*
*1 "If ye then be risen with Christ, seek those things which are above, where Christ sitteth on the right hand of God."*

*"Set your affection on things above, not on things on the earth."*
Have you ever been so focused upon a sight that you just couldn't turn away? Many people are like this when they pass an accident. Maybe when watching fireworks it's hard to turn away. I know my wife would probably say I'm like this when watching football!

The scriptures make it very clear that we are to set our heart on things above, on heaven. We can enjoy the things of earth, but our priority is to be heavenly in nature. We must long for the things of God to desire to make that our final goal—living for God and with Christ forever. Colossians 3:2 says to set your mind on things above, not on earthly things. Although we live in this earth our mind and hearts are to be on heaven and our eventual life there.

The eyes are the windows to your soul. They will only focus on things that are pleasing to your mind and heart. If your mind and heart are focused on heavenly issues, then your eyes will follow suit. Do not allow your eyes to change the focus of your heart or your desire for godly and heavenly tasks.

# You're Going To Spank Me?

*Proverbs 3:12*
*"For whom the Lord loveth he correcteth; even as a father the son in whom he delighteth."*

My daughter attended a Christian school for 14 years (K-4 through 12th grade). My brother Robert started the school for a local church and served as the school Administrator for many years. Carissa was a very good girl and rarely had to be corrected when growing up. She was a very spirited child and enjoyed life to its fullest. My sister Cathy was a teacher at the school. Carissa enjoyed the benefits of seeing family during the day and loved telling others about her family working at the school.

When Carissa was in K-5, the school had been in existence for two years. I don't remember the exact reason but she got into trouble in her class and was sent to the Administrator's office. Of course, she was glad to get to go to her uncle's office because she would go in there frequently to say hello and get candy or coins. My brother would give Carissa and her cousin all the change in his pocket whenever he saw them. So although she had violated a rule, she had no fear of the Administrator.

My brother spoke with her about what she did and how it was wrong. He then called me at work to explain the situation to me. He stated that the punishment would normally be one lick with the rod of correction (a big paddle he kept in his office) but he did not want to spank her. I told him she needed to be treated the same as other students and receive the required discipline. He was shocked but Carissa was more shocked! She looked at her uncle with big blue eyes and said, "You're going to spank me?" Robert replied that it was her dad's decision because he loves her. She received her one lick and has never forgotten! Carissa has the privileged distinction of being the first child to receive the rod of correction at the school (although it has since been discontinued). Her feelings were hurt more than her bottom, but she never repeated the offense.

Although we may be shocked, dismayed, and upset at God, He has the responsibility of disciplining His children. Each time we receive discipline it is because of our own actions. We cannot blame God or anyone else. God corrects us because He loves us. I had my daughter corrected because I loved her and wanted her to learn a lesson. She couldn't violate the rules thinking her uncle would protect her. She learned and never went back to his office again—except for the candy and change!

God's discipline is meant to cause a change in our behavior. It should be life-changing and produce a love for God's Word and His love for us. I know my daughter has never forgotten this experience and we still laugh at it to this very day. She now understands that true parental love demands correction to protect the individual from further harm and destruction.

# It's Going To Rain

*Genesis 6:6*
*"And it repented the Lord that he had made man on the earth, and it grieved him at his heart."*

God created man to have sweet, wonderful fellowship with Him. He desired to walk in the cool of the evening with man in the Garden of Eden. God gave man everything he needed to survive and created him to rule this world. He even saw that man was alone and decided to make him a companion—woman.

However, man sinned. He disobeyed God and was banished from the Garden of Eden. As a result of their sin, man was cursed, woman was cursed, the serpent was cursed, and even the earth and all of it was cursed. Men continued to sin and draw further away from God until the point God was looking for just one righteous person. "God was sorry that He had made man and He was grieved in His heart." So God vowed to destroy the earth and start over. But He needed one righteous man to rescue the human race and He chose Noah.

Noah was not the most talented, the most skilled, or had the highest social standing. But he was one who walked with God daily, listened to His voice, and followed the lead of the Lord. Noah was not perfect; he had his weaknesses, but he loved the Lord, was righteous in His eyes, and would obey the commandments of God.

Because of this loyalty, steadfastness in the Lord, and his righteousness, Noah was allowed to save his family and mankind from total destruction. He built an ark based on a promise from God even though he saw no rain. Upon completion of the ark, God called Noah and his family and the animals upon the ark because, just as God promised, "It is going to rain for forty days and forty nights."

This world that we live in is once again evil in the sight of the Lord. Mankind has turned from the Lord and is fulfilling the sins of the flesh without fear of retribution from the Lord. God is once again looking for the righteous that He can use to reach out to a lost and dying world. God is not going to destroy the world by flood, but He is going to come for a church without spot or wrinkle. A holy church that is living a righteous life and standing for Christ in a world that rejects Him.

God needs leaders who are willing to be His voice. He is not looking for the most talented, the most skilled, or those who have the best social standing. He is looking for one who walks with Him, listens to His voice, and will follow His commandments. Are you willing? Are you listening? Because metaphorically, I think it's about to rain again. . .

# Is This Heaven?

*Psalm 8:3-4*
*"When I consider thy heavens, the work of thy fingers, the moon and the stars, which thou hast ordained;"*
*"What is man, that thou art mindful of him? and the son of man, that thou visitest him?"*

Have you ever thought about what heaven will be like? I was fortunate enough to play golf on the Robert Trent Jones courses in Alabama. The course Capital Hill is located in Prattville, Alabama, and I remember the first time I played the course. From the very first hole, it is breathtaking. In the early morning, the sun is rising and there is dew just leaving the course. As you stand on the first tee you can see the Montgomery downtown skyline in the distance. The tee box is about 150 feet above the green. The green is surrounded on three sides by the Alabama River. You can hear birds, squirrels, and leaping cranes as they awake from their slumber. I asked my playing partner, "Is this heaven?" It was a perfect moment—until I started playing golf! Honestly, I would rather shoot the entire course with a camera instead of my clubs.

I'm sure heaven will be breathtaking and full of amazing sights. We see the wonders of this world through colored glass but when we see heaven our eyes will be made whole and we will see more unbelievable sights than ever before. But that is not our final destination. God is going to create a new heaven and a new earth that will be our everlasting home. A place where we will reign with Him forever!

I can't wait to see the improvements He has in store for my favorite golf course. . .

# I'm So Lucky To Know You

*1 Thessalonians 3:9*
*"For what thanks can we render to God again for you, for all the joy wherewith we joy for your sakes before our God."*

Do you seem to notice how coincidences keep happening to you? Or do you hear people say, "You're so lucky." Well, here is the scoop for you—God is in control of your life! Do you think it is just coincidence who your neighbors are? Is it just by luck that you met your spouse? Did you happen to "land" in your job because you are so talented? Please understand that God ordains the movements of your life. Yes, there are times that we royally mess up the great opportunities that God gives to us. But He continues to orchestrate the opportunity for greatness for us. Instead of giving luck credit for your blessings, thank God for His goodness and watchful eye.

# Let The Children Come

*Mark 10:14*
*"But when Jesus saw it, he was much displeased, and said unto them, Suffer the little children to come unto me, and forbid them not: for of such is the kingdom of God."*

What is it about children that we enjoy the most? Curiosity? Innocence? Playfulness? Sincerity? Lack of inhibition? You may appreciate other childlike qualities as well. I truly believe that God instills these traits in little ones and that is what we lose somehow, somewhere on our road to adulthood.

You notice how adults mostly want to dampen the enthusiasm children display? When they love, they show it! They run to you and want to hang on you and want you to pick them up so they can hug your neck really, really hard! Christ said, do not hinder them, and let them come unto me. He also said the kingdom of God belongs to such as these.

I remember when my daughter was a little girl. She would run to me yelling, "Daddy, daddy!" with her arms reaching out to me. I would grab her and she gave me big hugs for no reason except she loved me. She didn't want anything, wasn't trying to butter me up for anything. She was sincere and genuine.

This is what Christ wants from us, sincerely genuine worship and adoration. Be excited about being His child and in His presence. I believe we will all have these qualities when we get to heaven. We will worship Him because we "get to"!

# From Average To Extraordinary

*Psalm 16:11*
*"Thou wilt shew me the path of life: in thy presence is fullness of joy; at thy right hand there are pleasures for evermore."*

Once when traveling on a business trip, I arrived at my hotel tired and hungry. I checked in at the desk to receive my room key for an average, typical hotel room. Nothing fancy, but it had a bed and that was my next destination! The manager explained that they had accidentally given my reserved room to another guest. What? I was tired and ready for rest. Thankfully, before I could respond, the manager explained they had a lovely suite they were giving me for no extra charge! Awesome! I thanked the manager and he said that is not all, you can have room service on us. I was speechless. The suite was amazing with a king-sized bed, Jacuzzi tub, refrigerator, and all the amenities I could want.

Although to a much greater degree, going from this world to the next will be the best package upgrade of all! Our senses will be improved, our bodies will be healed, and our mission will be complete! There will be no temptation or sin to cause pain or death! I believe the food will be the best we've ever eaten!

Make sure you do everything possible to prepare for your final trip—and take as many people with you as possible!

# He Calls Them By Name

*Isaiah 40:26*
*"Lift up your eyes on high, and behold who hath created these things, that bringeth out their host by number: he calleth them all by names by the greatness of his might, for that he is strong in power; not one faileth."*

The older I get the harder it is to remember names, dates, and precious memories. My wife and family might ask if I remember a specific incident and they will have to give me more and more clues before I respond, "Oh, yes I remember!"

This verse declares that God created all of the heavens and the earth. Not only did He create them, He calls the stars by name! He keeps all of them in place.

There are stars that are so large that millions of our sun could fit into them. The distances are so great that we would have to travel millions of light-years just to reach them. Yet He keeps every star and planet in place by His word.

If we are truly amazed by the things of this world, just imagine what God has in store for us in the next world. Be sure to get your ticket before it is too late!

# Life Long Job Interview

*Romans 12:6*
*"Having then gifts differing according to the grace that is given to us, whether prophecy, let us prophesy according to the proportion of faith."*

Once we accept Christ that is the beginning of our new life with Him. We are to serve Him with the gifts and abilities given to us by Him. God is watching to see what we do with the gifts He has given us. The Word of God declares that the humble will be exalted (Luke 14:11) and those who can be trusted with little can also be trusted with much (Luke 16:10).

It's like you're on a job interview during this life for the next. God will determine your role in His kingdom on how you serve Him during your life on this earth. If you're faithful with what He gives you now, you can expect more responsibility in the new earth. If you just want to get by now then you may have little reward in the new kingdom.

All will be judged according to their works on this earth, both the sinner at the great white throne judgment and the saint at the marriage supper of the Lamb.

If you want the job of a lifetime in the new earth, then you better remember you are on your job interview right now.

# We Are Going To A Wedding!

*Revelation 19:9*
*"And he saith unto me, Write, Blessed are they which are called unto the marriage supper of the Lamb. And he saith unto me, These are the true sayings of God."*

Do you remember the wedding between Prince Charles and Princess Diana? Millions across the world watched and talked for weeks about the beauty and majesty of the wedding. What if you had been one of the very select to attend the wedding in person? How special would you have felt to be invited to the royal wedding of a lifetime?

I have great news! If you are a child of God you have a standing reservation to attend the most royal, holy, majestic wedding in the history of the entire universe—the marriage supper of the Lamb. Not only are you invited as a guest but you will be the bride prepared for the groom, Jesus Christ! The universe will be in attendance but they can only watch. You are invited as the one for whom the groom is throwing the wedding! "Blessed are these invited to the wedding supper of the Lamb."

What other motivation is needed to remain pure and holy before our God? Keep yourself from filth and sin and you will be at the center of the greatest wedding the universe will ever know!

# God's Presence

*Psalm 8:1*
*"O Lord, our Lord, how excellent is thy name in all the earth! who hast set thy glory above the heavens."*

Have you ever experienced the presence of God? Walking on a beach on an early summer day? Perhaps hiking through the mountains on a crisp fall afternoon? Staring into a clear, starry sky late one winter evening? Maybe even by looking into the eyes of a newborn baby? God can be found everywhere if you are searching for Him. His presence can be in the quiet breath of wind or in a loud roar of the ocean waves. He can be found in a moment of silence with only the cry of an eagle in the distance. Nature declares the glory and presence of God every day. Every sunrise and sunset is God's way of saying good morning and good night.

God's presence should be with you and in you every day. You may be the only Jesus that some will every see. How did you represent Him today to the world?

Some have said that God is boring—they do not know the God that I know! God is anything but boring. To know Him, you must seek Him. The more we seek the more He will reveal because we can never fully understand the things of God in this life. A child of God could never be bored with the knowledge that we have the honor of worshipping Jesus Christ and God the Father into eternity.

Now that's a worship service I do not want to miss!

# The Scriptures Are For Encouragement

*Romans 15:4*
*"For whatsoever things were written aforetime were written for our learning, that we through patience and comfort of the scriptures might have hope."*

The Bible tells us that once we accept Christ, we are new creatures. However, many times Satan will try to use our past to make us feel guilty or unworthy of God's love. The fact is that we have all sinned and fallen short of the glory of God. Whether you have broken one commandment or all of the Ten Commandments doesn't matter. You have sinned. I have sinned. But Satan will try to make you believe God will not forgive you of certain sins or failures in your life. That is a lie of Satan. "If you confess your sin, God is faithful and just to forgive you of your sins" (1 John 1:9). Your sins will be covered by the blood of Jesus and never to be remembered or mentioned again.

This does not give us liberty to continue in sin after accepting Christ (Romans 6:1-2). We are to forsake our sinful ways and to walk as Christ. God knows that we do not become perfect once we accept Him as our Lord and Savior. But our heart must be seeking after the Lord and our desire needs to be pleasing our heavenly Father every moment of every day.

So when you are feeling guilty, discouraged, or tempted of Satan to give up, just read the stories of all those who lived before us and how God used them in spite of their failures and sin. God uses the willing, the available, and those who are seeking to walk in His ways. If He only used perfect people, He would not have a church. Learn the Word. Love the Word. Live the Word. If you will, God certainly has a job for you!

# You Must Protect Your House!

*Psalm 101:3*
*"I will set no wicked thing before mine eyes: I hate the work of them that turn aside; it shall not cleave to me."*

There has been a commercial in the last few years about the home football team perfecting their home field advantage. The players are yelling, "We must protect this house!" It simply means we will not allow anyone to come into our house, push us around, and take victory from us.

Christians have the same challenge that we need to fulfill every day in our own homes. "We must protect this house!" should be our cry before the Lord. How many times do you allow vile scenes allowed into your home through television, movies, the internet, etc? This scripture declares that, "I will set before my eyes, no vile thing."

We are instructed to flee temptation through the power that Christ gives us. "Greater is He that is in us than he that is in the world" (1 John 4:4). By this power and God's wisdom, you can defeat any sin that tries to enter your home or life. This is one reason you have chosen to learn the verses in this book. To be able to discern right from wrong, His will for your life, and to have the ability to be victorious by quoting the Word of God.

This would be a great time to fast from television, study His Word, learn the scriptures and strengthen your spiritual man. Remember, it is up to you to protect your house from the vile things of this world.

# Candidate For Revival

*Jonah 1:1-3*
*"Now the word of the Lord came unto Jonah the son of Amittai, saying, Arise, go to Nineveh, that great city, and cry against it; for their wickedness is come up before me. But Jonah rose up to flee unto Tarshish from the presence of the Lord, and went down to Joppa; and he found a ship going to Tarshish: so he paid the fare thereof, and went down into it, to go with them unto Tarshish from the presence of the Lord."*

Imagine this scenario. Many of us say, "Lord, send me and use me as You will." God says, "Fine, go preach to your enemies about my love for them and that I want to save them." We answer, "But God, they have tortured your people and are a vicious and vile people. I don't want them to be saved!"

Have you ever felt this way? I've heard Christians say they hoped that Hitler, Stalin, serial rapists, or murderers didn't get saved before they died. God desires for all men to be saved. Even those who have rebelled against His will their entire lives. Hell was not meant for any person. Christians must have a strong desire to see everyone come to the saving grace of Jesus Christ, even the vilest offenders in our world.

Jonah ran from the calling to preach to the Assyrians. They were a ruthless people who tortured their captives just to scare others and to keep them from resisting their control. Jonah said, "No." God said, "Yes." Jonah ran from God and again said, "No." God sought Jonah and finally used a large fish to persuade him to say yes. Once Jonah went and preached the gospel, a great revival broke out and many were saved. Lives were changed.

God uses the willing to start revival. He also uses those who may be running from Him. God will take your "time in the wilderness" and use it to prepare you for your ministry to come. If you are not where you need to be with God, you may be running right into the arms of God. By the way, you may want to stay away from big fish during your rebellion to God!

# Drink From Your Own Well

*Proverbs 5:15*
*"Drink waters out of thine own cistern, and running waters out of thine own well."*

Ever been to a party? Usually when you have a group of people together you will get a glass and then put your name on it or mark it someway to ensure only you drink from your glass, and only you. Why? To protect yourself and others.

This verse is referencing your spouse. Drink from your own cistern, your own well. God ordained for us who are married to enjoy our spouse alone. Our spouse alone should provide the sexual satisfaction that is needed and desired. To do otherwise will only bring deception, sin, and embarrassment into your life. Protect your spouse and your love just as you would life-giving water. You definitely want your water pure, undefiled, and without filth.

If you do not have a marriage partner yet, then you should abstain from fulfilling this part of your life. Abstinence is not popular, but it is Biblical. Give all your love and affection unto the Lord until He will bring the right person into your life for marriage.

Protect the love source God has given you and it will provide a pure source of intimacy and comfort for a lifetime.

# Are You A Success ~ In God's Eyes?

*Matthew 7:21*
*"Not every one that saith unto me, Lord, Lord, shall enter into the kingdom of heaven; but he that doeth the will of my Father which is in heaven."*

How do you define success? The world would define success by how much money you have, how big your house or car is, the type of position you hold, or the amount of power you possess. Perhaps you are successful if you are known around the world or you're a best selling author. A gospel tract humorously summed it up this way—the one with the most toys wins!

God has a different standard of success. He defines true success as one who is obedient to Him. Only those who trust in the Lord and obey the will of God shall enter the kingdom of heaven.

I used to think the way of the world. I chased after bigger houses, promotions, money, and the ability to have many toys. I would say I needed to do it for my family. I was fooling myself. Our families would rather have us spend time with them and enjoy them instead of working excessive hours a week to get them another toy. Give your family the gift of you rather than worrying about worldly goods and desires.

God will be the one to ultimately decide if you have been successful or not. I believe He will look at how many people you witnessed to? How many of the poor did you help? Did you use the gifts He gave you to minister to the body of Christ?

Your true success can only be measured by spiritual standards and God will reward those who diligently seek Him.

# You Have Been Warned

*"For I testify unto every man that heareth the words of the prophecy of this book, If any man shall add unto these things, God shall add unto him the plagues that are written in this book."*

God is very protective about His word. This scripture is a warning not to add, delete, or change His word. He gave it to us just the way He meant to. God also warns His people that in the last days there will be false religions, fake prophets, and false interpretations.

Beware of those coming with "new" revelation. God gave us His revelation in the Holy Bible. There is not a new one from our God today. Religions and false teachers will use the word of God but then add to it or use it incorrectly to benefit them. They will come to "tickle your ears" rather than preach the true word of God. Why? Many would not be able to build the large congregations or collect large sums of money if they preached the gospel of accountability, of picking up your cross and following Christ, and repenting of your sins to be saved.

Some who use the title "pastor" think of the church only as a business. Church members are seen as customers and Jesus as an icon to pull people into the church. The message is all about love, grace, prosperity, land of promise, every need met with no suffering or sacrifice. That is a false message.

Stay true to the real message of the Bible and the Jesus of the Bible. Do not be swayed or let your ears be tickled for the Bible says many saints will fall away in the last days. We have been warned.

# He Is Always With You

*Ephesians 4:30*
*"And grieve not the holy Spirit of God, whereby ye are sealed unto the day of redemption."*

In our city there were certain intersections where drivers would frequently run through the red lights. This was very dangerous and caused many accidents and even deaths. So the city decided to put up red light cameras to discourage this behavior. Did it work? Yes! Once people knew they were being watched they stopped running red lights. This led to fewer accidents and fatalities. Why did the camera make a difference? Because people knew that someone would be watching and there would be consequences to their actions.

Do you know that your entire life is being recorded? The Holy Spirit is with you every second of every day. He sees, hears, and watches everything you say and do. There is no hiding place from God. You can hide activities from your friends, neighbors, and even family, but God knows it all. Then one day as you stand before God and Christ your entire life will be played back for the saints to see. Wow!

Repent and turn away from your sin. Do not grieve the Holy Spirit of God, for He is burdened and hurt every time you decide to serve self and flesh rather than Him. If you were to keep this one thought before you every day, how could you ever sin again?

Turn your eyes upon Jesus and don't look back for God is definitely watching you.

# Have You Seen The Risen Lord?

*John 20:20*
*"And when he had so said, he shewed unto them his hands and his side. Then were the disciples glad, when they saw the Lord."*

The disciples of the Lord were called to follow Him, and they did. During the three years of Jesus' ministry, they were learning, doubting, and questioning just about as much as everyone else. Jesus knew that would happen. He was okay with knowing they had to learn what His kingdom was all about this time around.

But after His death and resurrection the disciples were different. Once Christ ascended, they preached mightily, and they went to the ends of the earth to be a witness for Christ. They performed miracles and planted churches. They were even willing to die horrible deaths all for the sake of Jesus.

What made the difference? They got a glimpse of the risen Lord! He died but He rose again! That was all it took to get them to sell out to the Lord 100%! They were willing to proclaim Him even unto death because they knew death could not hold them or keep them. Christ had defeated death and hell on the cross and by rising up from the dead Himself.

Have you caught a glimpse of the risen Lord? If not, now is the time to realize He is not just a sweet baby in a manger, or just a good man, or just a great teacher. He is the Son of God! He died and was resurrected for us so we could have everlasting life with Him and His Father.

If you have seen the risen Lord, then proclaim the good news to every part of your world! Be bold in the Lord for there is nothing this world can do to you to harm you. Proclaim, "I have seen the risen Lord!"

# God's Blessing Is Conditional

*Proverbs 11:1*
*"A false balance is abomination to the Lord: but a just weight is his delight."*

How many times have you tried to take a shortcut and it ended up being longer than the normal route? Many of us try to bring our own blessings even though it may not be the most honorable way. Have you ever left work early without permission? Called in sick when you were feeling fine? Buy something from an individual for an extremely low price but didn't worry about where it came from?

My friend was a season ticket holder for a state football team. He asked if I wanted his two seats for a specific game. I said, "Sure, my daughter loves going to football games with her dad!" There was an event being held before the game for season ticket holders only, and he said all I had to do was use his name to get in. Although I really wanted to go, would that have been the honorable thing to do? I politely refused. My friend meant no harm and just wanted to do me a favor. But God cannot bless unless we walk in His character.

If you are not walking according to His word and His will for your life, He cannot bless you. You have handcuffed the blessings of God in your life. Don't believe God will bless good talk. He wants to see us "walk the walk" as well.

# Quit? Or Try Again?

James 1:3-4
*"Knowing this, that the trying of your faith worketh patience. But let patience have her perfect work, that ye may be perfect and entire, wanting nothing."*

I have counseled many couples about marital issues. No marriage is fail proof or without problems. The first thing I ask both parties is, "Do you want to be here?" There is nothing worse than someone sitting in counseling who does not want to be there. Their mind is made up and there is a stone wall around their mind. One couple in particular both said they wanted to be there. But they were so full of bitterness and doubt that both didn't believe anything could help them. I said to the couple, if you don't believe, then just quit and go your separate ways. They both asked me, "Are you supposed to say that?" I told them to quit or try again, but this time you must make it work. They began to listen. When there is no other option, your marriage will work. Too many people look at every other option and say, "This is my parachute whenever I want out."

Life's tough choices have two options. Quit, or keep going. Quit and you usually regret the decision, become bitter or full of resentment. I can guarantee you this — once you quit, you'll always see that as your first option from that moment on. Or, you can keep going. You can persevere, let the testing of your faith mold your character. Perseverance brings forth maturity. Maturity will bring forth completion.

The couple I was counseling took quitting out of their vocabulary and resolved their differences by the Word of God! They found that their perseverance brought forth maturity in their marriage, and they have a complete marriage through living the principles of the Word of God every day.

# Make Your Failures Count

*2 Corinthians 1:3-4*
*"Blessed be God, even the Father of our Lord Jesus Christ, the Father of mercies, and the God of all comfort; Who comforteth us in all our tribulation, that we may be able to comfort them which are in any trouble, by the comfort wherewith we ourselves are comforted of God."*

Failure is a part of life. If you have never failed, then you have not tried anything new. The problem is not failing at something—it is how you respond to your failures. Hopefully, you will learn from your failures and not repeat them. However, some people have to repeat failures in life to learn the lesson God is trying to teach them.

Jus as God is present to comfort us in the midst of our troubles and failures, He wants us to be available to others during their times of failure. God allows us to experience disappointments in life for several reasons. First, we learn more during times of trial than times of success. If we have nothing but success, then we become self-dependent and begin to believe we can do this without God. Secondly, He teaches us about His compassion and hopefully we will show others the same compassion we received from Him.

Give God glory in every situation and ask Him, "What is it you want to teach me?" Be content with whatever you have and in whatever circumstances you find yourself. If you are His child, then God is in control, and everything works to the good for those who are called according to His purpose.

"And we know that all things work together for good to them that love God, to them who are the called according to his purpose" (Romans 8:28).

# Have You Been Cursed Today?

*1 Peter 4:14*
*"If ye be reproached for the name of Christ, happy are ye; for the spirit of glory and of God resteth upon you: on their part he is evil spoken of, but on your part he is glorified."*

The great minister John Wesley knew what it meant to be persecuted for Christ's sake. His message was so strong and filled with the Spirit of God that as he would preach, people would throw vegetables, fruit, and other objects at him. In his journal, he once wrote that he was blessed because he had only been assaulted one time that day!

All of the disciples were persecuted daily. Many Christians in the world today face persecution and even death for holding church services or just mentioning the name of Christ. A survey was taken asking Christians in America why they do not witness to others about Christ? The number one answer was fear—the fear of being rejected, ridiculed, or mocked. I believe Christians have their fear rooted in the wrong place. Christ said, "If you deny me before men, I will deny you before my Father in heaven" (Matthew 10:33). We should have fear of the Lord more than the fear of men. Men may laugh at us, curse us, or even ridicule us—but if we deny Christ, God will deny us and cast us into the lake of fire. Which is worse?

If you are insulted because of Christ, the Word says you are blessed because the Spirit of glory and of God rests on you.

If you are not being cursed or chastised for Christ, then maybe you are not a threat to the kingdom of Satan.

# How Full Is Your Love Tank?

*1 Corinthians 13:13*
*"And now abideth faith, hope, charity, these three; but the greatest of these is charity."*

The theme of the Bible is love. God's love, the love of Christ, a brother's love, the love of a friend, and love one for another. Romans 13:8 states, "Let no debt remain outstanding, except the continuing debt to love one another." If you want answers to your prayers, you must love. If you want effectual faith, you must love others. Love is the foundation for everything God has designed for us.

Love —

-- endures long and is slow to lose patience.

-- is kind.

-- does not envy and is not jealous.

-- does not boast and is not anxious to impress.

-- is not proud or arrogant.

-- has good manners and is not rude.

-- does not gratify self or insist on its own way.

-- is not touchy or easily angered.

-- keeps no record of wrongs.

-- never delights in evil.

-- rejoices with the truth.

-- has no limit to its endurance.

-- always trusts and is ready to believe the best.

-- never loses hope.

-- always perseveres and can outlast anything.

-- never fails or comes to an end.

# Does the Enemy Have A Stronghold in You?

*John 14:30*
*"Hereafter I will not talk much with you: for the prince of this world cometh, and hath nothing in me."*

Jesus lived the perfect life. Many say it was easy for Him because He was God! He was God but He was fully human as well. He faced the same challenges and temptations that you and I do. But He never allowed the devil an opportunity to influence His life.

You need to break your alliance with the devil and any stronghold he has in your life. Commit your life to God fresh every morning, and confess your sins to the Lord so they may be put under the blood of Christ. You cannot bury your sin. It must all be confessed by you unto the Lord so Satan has nothing in you.

Are you still harboring unforgiveness toward anyone? Have you committed a wrong against another but have not asked their forgiveness? Do you have doubt, fear, resentment, or unresolved anger you have not dealt with? Is Satan still using past sins, failure, idolatry (putting anything before God) or laziness to keep you from fulfilling God's call on your life?

Pray right now. Confess all of your sins before God. Have nothing of the enemy within your life and be filled with the Spirit of God!

# A Divided Kingdom Will Fall

*Matthew 12:25*
*"And Jesus knew their thoughts, and said unto them, Every kingdom divided against itself is brought to desolation; and every city or house divided against itself shall not stand."*

Have you noticed how divided our nation is? Just about every poll that comes out, no matter the question, the answer is just about a 50/50 split. Republican, Democrat, abortion, economy, social issues, government regulations, foreign policy, etc. Our country has been divided in everything. Even the main philosophy our country is based upon—Christianity—is being attacked and eliminated from the public life of Americans.

The Bible proclaims that in the last days, kingdoms will be divided against themselves, even cities and households would be divided. 2 Timothy 3:1-5 states, "People will be lovers of themselves, lovers of money, boastful, proud, abusive, disobedient to their parents, ungrateful, unholy, without love, unforgiving, slanderous, without self control, brutal, not lovers of the good, treacherous, rash, conceited, lovers of pleasure rather than lovers of God—having a form of godliness but denying its power. Have nothing to do with them."

Does this sound like our world today? Satan's goal is to divide. Divide countries, families, couples, churches, races, schools, businesses, work areas—wherever there are people!

We must recognize the spirit of separation; renounce it in your life. The battle is one of the spirit and not of the flesh (Ephesians 6:12). Remember to start with yourself. Get rid of all self-centeredness and stubbornness. Restore unity within your own life and pray for God to move in these last days.

# What Are You Teaching Your Child?

Proverbs 22:6
"*Train up a child in the way he should go: and when he is old, he will not depart from it.*"

Children are a gift from God. The Bible speaks much about the qualities of a child and how they are a blessing of the Lord. Christ even said that we are to be like little children when approaching the kingdom of God. The Bible says we are to correct our children, use the rod of corrections and not to hate them. "He that spareth his rod hateth his son: but he that loveth him chasteneth him betimes" (Proverbs 13:24).

I'm sure every parent can remember the first time they looked into their child's eyes. Remember holding them for the very first time? I remember seeing my daughter for the very first time. It was a Wednesday and it felt like time stood still. She was so beautiful, so small! I remember praying at that moment, "Lord, she is yours. I commit her to you to do with as you please." As the earthly parents to our children it is our job to teach them everything. Teach them how to walk, talk, what to touch, not to touch, how to play ball, study, sing, everything. But the most important thing we can teach our children are the things of God. Teach them His work, His love, His salvation plan for us, His power, majesty and forgiveness. Start this training when they are young and they will not leave it later in life.

I'm so proud that my daughter loves the Lord! She is a child of God, active in ministry, studying His Word, and waiting for a godly man to be faithful to in the future. I love Carissa with all of my heart and I'm so proud of her and the godly woman she has become.

If your child is not saved then keep praying and believing for God to save them. Tell your children how much you love them and are praying for them.

# Refreshing Water

*Matthew 11:28*
*"Come unto me, all ye that labor and are heavy laden, and I will give you rest."*

I try to run as often as possible. Ever since running in a half-marathon last year, my wife and I go to a local park and exercise. She walks due to having knee surgery, and I try to jog at least three miles every time I'm out. It really helps to keep the weight off and I feel much better when I exercise daily.

During the summer it is really hard to stay committed to exercise due to the Southern summer heat. As I'm running I'm sweating, getting very tired, and the heat becomes unbearable. But I press on. I'm tempted to stop and allow the excuses to begin. "It's too hot. I've gone far enough for today." But I keep going to the end of my route and finally finish strong. I rush home to find refreshment in my swimming pool! I change and jump right in to a refreshing, cool, and relaxing pool of water. I stay under the water for as long as I can to let the water cover me and refresh me.

When you become tired and exhausted from the trials and burdens of this world, Christ is the refreshing water that you need. He says if you are weary, tired, burdened (carrying a large weight upon you), then come unto Him and He will give you rest. He will set before you a refreshing pool of water that you can soak in to renew your strength. He loves you and cares for you. No matter your trial, He is greater! Put your trust in Jesus Christ your Lord.

# Whom Do You Serve?

Joshua 24:15
*"And if it seem evil unto you to serve the Lord, choose you this day whom ye will serve; whether the gods which your fathers served that were on the other side of the flood, or the gods of the Amorites, in whose land ye dwell: but as for me and my house, we will serve the Lord."*

My wife and I have many activities that we enjoy together. We love to take a motorcycle ride through the country. We work out together in the gym, the park, the living room, wherever is convenient. We love cooking and eating together! We enjoy a good game of "chicken foot" dominoes with friends. We most certainly enjoy having family over and hearing how God is moving in their lives.

Most importantly, we love serving our Lord. We enjoy fellowship with our home church family. We enjoy worshipping God by singing with the choir and praise team. We attend a wonderful Sunday School class and have an excellent pastor who teaches the true word of God.

If you were to take an audit of your family's activities, finances, and commitments, where would your heart be? Would people know you are a Christian family? Do your neighbors and co-workers know that you have chosen to serve God?

In a world of idols, with people turning from the true God, Joshua made a bold proclamation to the Nation of Israel, "Serve whom you will, but for me and my house, we will serve the Lord!"

Decide today to make God the Lord of your family every single day that He gives you to serve Him.

# Mommy, Mickey Mouse is Calling!

*John 10:27*
*My sheep hear my voice, and I know them, and they follow me...*

We were able to take our daughter, Carissa, to Disney World when she was about six years old. She loved every minute of the trip! She was able meet all of her favorite Disney characters, such as Pluto, Goofy, Mickey and Minnie Mouse, Cinderella, and so many more. She had her autograph book and had each "star" sign their name. When I saw her face as she met those characters and got to speak to them and hug them, I knew it was an expression I will never forget. To see her so happy was worth the entire trip.

When we arrived home, Carissa kept talking about the trip. She carried her autograph book with her everywhere, showing everyone. One day, I really don't know why, I decided to call my daughter on the phone using the voice of Mickey Mouse. She answered the phone, and I said, "Hello, is Carissa there? This is Mickey Mouse calling!" Carissa became really excited. "Hi, Mickey, I'm Carissa!" "Hello, Carissa, Minnie and I miss you and want you to know we loved getting to meet you." Carissa yelled to her mom, "Mom, it's Mickey Mouse on the phone! He called me!" When I got home that is all she could talk about. I called many times throughout the year and she loved it. Years later I finally told her it was me. We laugh about those calls even to this day. She will call me and say, "Dad, do the Mickey voice."

There are many voices that try to get our attention today. We must know our shepherd's voice and stay close to Him. Although I called my daughter for a pleasant reason, many voices today are trying to lead us away from our true Father. Many voices may sound appealing but will only lead down a path of destruction. Follow your Father's voice and He will always lead you down the path of righteousness.

# What Did You Say?!

*Galatians 5:17*
*For the flesh lusts against the Spirit, and the Spirit against the flesh; and these are contrary to one another, so that you do not do the things that you wish.*

I have a cousin nicknamed Butch. When we were young, Butchie would come to my house to stay overnight. My father was a very strict disciplinarian. If you remember the show *Gomer Pyle, USMC*, my dad was just like the character Sgt. Carter. Many a Saturday morning we heard, "move it, move it, move it!"

Butchie and I were playing in the backyard one day. It was getting late and near suppertime when my dad came to the door and yelled, "I told you boys to come inside to eat!" My cousin said, "Shut up!" I looked at him, my mouth dropped open, and I knew what was coming next. My dad threw open the door so hard that I thought it would come off the hinges. He came toward us like a bull charging at a red cape! His eyes were bulging and I even think smoke was coming out of his eyes! He came within six inches of Butchie and yelled, "What did you say?!" Butchie stood there frozen and replied with as much strength as he could muster, "I don't know, but it wasn't shut up." My dad replied, "I didn't think so. Get inside for supper." As he walked into the house Butch looked at me and said, "I love Uncle Bobby, even if he is mean!"

There are times we do things we just know are crazy. The flesh gets the best of us. Commit yourself to God, and train your spirit and your flesh in the ways of God. He stills loves you when you fail or disappoint Him. Don't give up on God or yourself. Fight the good fight every day, and our heavenly Father will be there for you every step of the way.

# Hearing Or Listening?

*Proverbs 18:13*
*He who answers a matter before he hears it, It is folly and shame to him.*

In the book *Leadership Challenge*, I read the following quote, "Seek to understand before being understood." Many people are so busy trying to get their point of view across that they aren't trying to understand the point of view of others. Think of the last time you were in a disagreement with someone. While they were telling you their view on the issue, were you truly listening or thinking about what you were going to say in your response to them? Admit it. Most of us do it. We must truly listen to know how to respond.

Men and women think differently on the issue of communication. Men want answers and solutions to problems. They want to state an issue and get it resolved as quickly as possible. Men usually do not discuss any issue they feel they can fix themselves. Women want to talk through an issue, receive assurance they are being heard, but are not always asking for an answer or a "fix" to a problem. Women usually like to discuss an issue even if they know they will resolve it themselves.

The Word of God tells us that the one who answers before listening has shame. You need to truly listen to others to be able to efficiently minister to their needs. This should start at home. Listen to your wife, your children, and others in your family who need your counsel. Once you seek to understand before being understood then you will remove shame from your life. You will then become the person others will want to seek for wise counsel for troubles in their lives.

# Can J Get A Witness!

Acts 26:28
*Then Agrippa said to Paul, "You almost persuade me to become a Christian."*

When was the last time you led someone to Christ? When was the last time you shared your testimony? God makes it clear that we are responsible for sharing the good news of Jesus Christ to every person. He is responsible for the harvest. You may never see one person accept Christ as his Lord and Savior, but if you are planting the seeds then you are being faithful to your calling in the Lord.

In Acts chapter 26, Paul is standing in court before King Agrippa. When Paul is permitted to speak, he begins giving his testimony. He testifies of the goodness of God, the life and resurrection of Christ, his conversion and calling from Jesus. King Agrippa replies, "You almost persuade me to become a Christian!"

You should be prepared to give your testimony at any time, sharing how Christ saved you, the demand of the law, the power of grace, and the death and resurrection of Jesus. Charles Spurgeon stated, "If you are not concerned with winning others for Christ and snatching them from the gates of hell, then I, Sir, have to question your conversion to Christ."

A prominent American physicist told this story years ago -- "I know friends who profess to know Christ. They attend church regularly and confess to believe one must accept Jesus as Lord and Savior or go to hell. Yet, not one of these friends has told me personally the good news of Christ. This must mean one of two things: either they don't like me and want me to go to hell, which I doubt; or they don't have strong convictions in their own beliefs. To believe and not try to save others must be the greatest sin of all." I couldn't say it better myself.

# Unity Through Humility

*Philippians 2:9,10,11*
*Therefore God also has highly exalted Him and given Him the name which is above every name, that at the name of Jesus every knee should bow, of those in heaven, and of those on earth, and of those under the earth, and that every tongue should confess that Jesus Christ is Lord, to the glory of God the Father.*

Do you believe God is in control? Many times when I try to make something happen in my life, I mess it up. Yes, we must be diligent for God to bless. However, we must remember that God should be in control of every situation. If we believe that we can accomplish tasks on our own, that only leads to pride and separation from God and our fellow man.

In Philippians chapter 2, Paul is using Jesus as the ultimate example of servant leadership. He reminds his audience they must be humble and not live selfishly (v. 2-4). He then reminds them of Christ's incarnation proving that the ultimate healer made the ultimate sacrifice. Christ left heaven, become a man. He left the highest of positions to become the lowest form of creation. Yet because of his humility and sacrifice, the scriptures declare that God gave him a name above names. At the mention of the name of Jesus, every knee shall bow and every tongue shall confess that Jesus Christ is Lord (v. 9-11). All of this was completed for one purpose -- to glorify God the Father!

Wherever God leads you in your life, your job, your church, serve to the best of your ability. Have humility and know that God gives advancement. God promotes in His time. If you are faithful in the small things then God will give you more responsibility.

# Finish What You Start

*2 Timothy 4:7*
*I have fought the good fight, I have finished the race, I have kept the faith.*

How many diets have you started and not finished? How many New Year's resolutions were broken even before the calendar saw February? Americans have a hard time finishing. Many do not count the cost before embarking on their journey. Once you commit to Christ, have the determination to go all the way with Him. Commit yourself fully unto God and His work.

Paul is speaking with urgency in his last epistle to Timothy. He doesn't waste his words with stories or examples. He gets right to the point and tells us what is most important to him. Paul states that we should have these priorities in our life.

Paul issues a challenge in front of God, who will judge the living and the dead at His appearing, to preach the Word! Preach with conviction, urgently, and at all times! Telling others of Christ must be the most important priority in your life. Be ready at all times to preach the Word! Preach the Word of God to convince, rebuke, and exhort (v. 12).

Paul proclaims to do the work of an evangelist. The day is here that Paul was teaching about. He said there will come a day when people will rebuke sound doctrine, go after their own desires, have itching ears, and turn from the truth. They will find teachers to proclaim to them the gospel they want to hear. That day is here, my friend! All the signs are present that Jesus is coming soon for His bride, the Church (v. 3-5).

Finally, Paul says to run the race to the end. Fight a good fight and keep the faith. If you do, you will receive a crown of righteousness. This is one race you definitely want to finish! (v. 6-8).

# Which Takes More Faith?

*Hebrews 11:3*
*By faith we understand that the worlds were framed by the word of God, so that the things which are seen were not made of things which are visible.*

In the beginning, God created the heavens and the earth. Simple enough, right? Scientists cannot accept this fact. They had rather have us believe that everything was created from nothing through some big bang. It's called the Big Bang Theory because it cannot be proven. They want us to accept that humans evolved over millions of years from some random cells. It's called Evolution Theory because it cannot be proven.

The fact is we know that every created thing must have a creator. Hebrews 11:3 states, "By faith we understand that the worlds were framed by the Word of God so that the things which are seen were not made of things which are invisible." Go back to verse one: "Now faith is the substance of things hoped for, the evidence of things not seen."

God makes it very clear He is the creator and author of all things -- the universe, galaxies, stars, mankind, all of it. The worlds were "framed," meaning put into place with order. We accept this by faith because we believe the living Word of God.

My house was a creation and had to have a creator. It didn't just have an explosion and every detail fall into proper place. Skyscrapers do not just evolve. They are the creation of a creator. God is our creator. He is the author and finisher of our faith.

We have a choice. Believe everything was put in perfect place by some random explosion, or believe the earth and mankind had a creator who is the same God who loves you and me. Which takes more faith?

# Everything Changes, But . . .

*Hebrews 13:8*
*Jesus Christ is the same yesterday, today, and forever.*

"The only thing constant is change itself." Everything changes. Years ago I really enjoyed electronics. I would buy the latest computer, phone, CD/DVD player, and television, and I thought I had the best out there. This one will last me forever! Then, not even six months later, a newer model would come out. I just couldn't keep up with the "newer, better than ever, more options and services" products that companies kept pushing to the consumer.

I've since become a little wiser to understand why companies need to push the newer, improved, better than ever, models. They want more of my money! I don't need a new phone, TV, or player, or anything else, until the one I have no longer meets my needs.

I am so thankful that Jesus Christ is the same yesterday, today, and forever! The God of Abraham is our God. The Jesus at the well is still giving life-changing water to our generation. The Jesus who died for our sins 2000 years ago is alive today to minister to our needs, and He is at the right hand of the Father interceding for you and me. The same loving, healing Jesus in my grandfather's sermons fifty years ago still performs miracles today.

Jesus will never need to be improved and He will never change. He is the same yesterday, today, and forever!

# Believing Is Not Enough

*James 2:19*
*You believe that there is one God. You do well. Even the demons believe--and tremble!*

Let's say two men were walking in the woods. As they came to a clearing, there was a river fifty feet below the level where they were standing. The only way to cross the river was to use the bridge that connects the two sides together. One man says to the other, "We must cross the bridge to the other side." The other man says, "I believe there is a bridge; I just don't trust it to get me to the other side." You can believe that something exists without believing in what it does.

While I was sharing the gospel with various people I have heard many a man say, "I believe there is a God." I would tell them, "That is wise because even the demons believe and tremble!" Not only do demons believe there is a God, but they fear God! Men may believe there is a God, but they do not fear Him. If they did, they would turn from their wicked ways and stop sinning before the Lord God. They would repent of their selfishness before it is too late.

How close are you to Judgment Day? Just one heartbeat! One heartbeat separates us from all eternity. Accept Jesus today before it is too late! Believe. Receive. Don't be deceived!

# Everyone Picks On The Baby

*Matthew 6:14*
*"For if you forgive men their trespasses, your heavenly Father will also forgive you.*

I am the youngest of four children. My brother Robert is twelve years older than I am, my sister Carole is nine years older, and my sister Cathy is six years older (five-and-a-half, according to her). They always enjoyed picking on their baby brother. There are many examples I could share but I'll stick to just one.

When I was around four years old we lived in a small house where all of the bedrooms, the bathroom, and the living room all opened into a rectangular hallway. My wonderful brother and sisters would put me in the hallway, turn out the light, and shut the doors. Now, as if this weren't enough fun, they would open one of the doors, turn on the light, and then chase me with a large stuffed moose head! I would run and scream while they were laughing, having a good old time. I don't know how long this went on, but it certainly hasn't left my memory! I'm just thankful I lived to see age five with all of that going on. Where they found an old stuffed moose head is another story altogether, and I won't tell you all the pranks they pulled on each other.

I forgave them of their scare tactics. I'm sure as I got older I did things to them that they had to forgive as well. Children do the funniest things. We joke about the fact that my brother and I both grew up to be psychologists/counselors.

The point is, we love each other, and we forgive those we love. However, the Word of God says to forgive everyone, not just the ones we love but also the unlovable, and even those who don't love us, so we can receive His forgiveness. We must forgive to be forgiven.

Robert, Carole Anne, and Cathy -- I forgive you, but . . . don't ever bring a moose head to my house!

# Be A Lion Hunter!

*1 Peter 5:8*
*Be sober, be vigilant; because your adversary the devil walks about like a roaring lion, seeking whom he may devour.*

I had always wondered what it would be like to go on an African safari. I imagined hunting the big game and bringing home a huge trophy from the hunt. I began watching television shows about big game hunting. What I learned was -- I don't really want to go big game hunting! While watching a program about hunting lions in particular, I discovered I might start out as the hunter but could end up being the one being hunted!

Lions are cunning, intelligent hunters. They can track their prey from long distances and are patient and diligent, willing to wait long hours for a chance at supper. If you plan to hunt a lion, the documentary stated, you had better stay alert. You really think so!? I decided to take up golf instead.

The scriptures state that we must remain sober. This means alert, awake to our surroundings. Do not be lulled asleep and lose your focus or concentration. We are also to be vigilant. This means to be prepared, on the lookout for any signs of trouble. As Christians, we must be alert and on the lookout for the lies of the devil. Peter said that Satan walks about like a roaring lion seeking whom he may devour. But do not be afraid for we have everything we need to defeat this adversary! We are to resist him and he will flee from us every time. Satan might try to deceive us, but we know who is victorious in the end.

Here kitty, kitty, kitty . . .

# Works That Last

*James 4:14*
*Whereas you do not know what will happen tomorrow. For what is your life? It is even a vapor that appears for a little time and then vanishes away.*

I was a youth pastor for many years. I remember one evening when we were gathered for a service and I asked everyone what plans they had for the future. One young man stated he was going to play professional football. Another stated he wanted to lead his own band. One young woman said she wanted to marry and have many children. There were answers of going to college, having a specific career, and falling in love.

I asked the students how many of them wanted to be remembered for what they accomplish on Earth? They all said yes. Do you want to be remembered for your earthly accomplishments?

The best investment you can make to ensure your work will be remembered is to win souls for Christ. Sure, you can build big skyscrapers and they will be gone in a hundred years or so. You could be the sweetest singer this world has ever known and have a career of forty or fifty years. You may even be remembered for a hundred years or more. But the best way to ensure you are remembered is to win souls. Why? Because those souls will live forever and ever. They will be a living testimony to your work and they will always remember who introduced them to Christ. What a legacy!

If you want to do an eternal work, something that you will receive rewards for from the God of the universe, share your testimony! Proclaim the good news! Jesus is Lord and He is coming back for His bride very soon.

# Things That Confound

*1 Corinthians 1:27*
*But God has chosen the foolish things of the world to put to shame the wise,*
*and God has chosen the weak things of the world to put to shame the things*
*which are mighty;*

The Israelites had been seeking a king for generations, a king who would deliver them and take revenge on their enemies. They had read the prophecies over and over and longed for the time their Messiah would come to deliver them.

God uses the unusual to confound the wise. He rarely works in the way we expect or even desire Him to meet our needs. God used plagues to get Pharaoh to let His people go out of Egypt. He used the Red Sea to defeat the Egyptian army. God told Joshua to march around Jericho seven days and the city would be delivered to him. God used a young boy named David to defeat the warrior giant Goliath, and He used Daniel to show that He even controls the mouths of lions.

Could God do things in a simple way? Sure, but that would be our way. God has a greater purpose in everything He does. He is far ahead of where we would be in meeting our own needs.

God answered the Israelites by sending the Messiah. But instead of a fighting warrior, God sent a baby. A baby? God knew what was needed to redeem not just the Israelites but all of mankind. He sent a savior, a Lamb of God who would die for the sins of the world. This same Jesus will come again with His saints and will eventually defeat all the enemies of Israel once and for all. Then there will be peace over all the earth and God's people will rejoice.

So don't be surprised when God answers your prayers and the answer comes in a completely different way than you expect. Thank God for His faithfulness and His love for His children.

# God Has A Plan for Your Life

*2 Kings 7:6*
*For the Lord had caused the army of the Syrians to hear the noise of chariots*
*and the noise of horses--the noise of a great army; so they said to one another,*
*"Look, the king of Israel has hired against us the kings of the Hittites and*
*the kings of the Egyptians to attack us!"*

Do you ever feel defeated? Discouraged? Like God has forgotten you? Everyone has been there. Remember, God has a plan for your life. If you are walking in the will of God then you are exactly where you need to be. Perhaps it's not the situation you would choose for yourself, but better to be a soldier in God's army than the General in your own.

In 2 Kings 7, the Israelites are under siege by the Syrian army. The city is barricaded and there are four lepers sitting outside the gates. The great Syrian army is camped just outside the city waiting to attack the Israelites. These four lepers had a choice to make. Because of the siege on the city there was a great famine. There was no food anywhere. Usually people would give leftovers to the lepers as they entered and exited the city gates, but no one was leaving or entering the city. The lepers could sit there and starve to death, or they could go to the camp of the Syrians and beg for food, knowing there was a great chance they would be killed.

Have you ever felt like those were your only choices -- "bad" and "worse"? Perhaps your choice is between paying your bills and feeding your family, or doing the right thing at work and losing your job if you do -- tough choices that force us to ask God if He knows what He is doing. This is where verse 6 comes into play. The lepers went to the enemy's camp and God "caused the Syrian army to hear the clatter of speeding chariots and the galloping of horses and the sounds of a great army approaching." This caused the Syrian army great fear and they fled from the camp wildly into the night!

God used these four lepers to defeat the Syrian army and they didn't have a clue that God was using them! Get this -- the Syrian army was defeated by a soundtrack! No actual army, no horses, no chariots, just the sounds of a great army! As four men approached the camp, they heard the sounds of a vast army. Amazing! Our God can do anything to defeat our enemies. Why do we doubt the power of God and His ability to use us and to deliver us in our time of need?

You might not like your current situation. There have been many times in my life when I asked God "why" I was in a particular test in my life. Sometimes He placed me there, and sometimes I put myself there through sin, pride, unbelief, or disobedience to Him. Either way, God is faithful and just to deliver us from our enemies and even ourselves.

Trust God. Pray and ask God to deliver you from your circumstances. Like Paul in prison, He might leave you there for a purpose. Like Job, He might be trying to teach faithfulness or patience. Like Christ, He might have a great purpose for your life that through your sacrifice and obedience you can change the world for Him. Remember, the worst thing that this world can do to you is kill you. That act just ushers you into the presence of the Lord where you will spend eternity worshipping God the Father and our Savior, the Lord Jesus Christ.

Keep the faith and remember that God is in control!

# God, I Am Not Worthy

*Isaiah 64:6*
*But we are all like an unclean thing, And all our righteousnesses are like filthy rags; We all fade as a leaf, And our iniquities, like the wind, Have taken us away.*

Many people believe they have to be perfect to be used of God. If that were true, who could go? None of us is perfect in God's eyes. All of us have sin in our lives. We were born that way. Even our righteous acts are like filthy rags before God. There is no way for us to obtain righteousness on our own.

Even those in the Bible who we read about accomplishing much for God were marred with sin. Moses was a murderer, King David was an adulterer, and Solomon eventually gave in to idolatry and worshipped the gods of his foreign wives. Matthew was a shady tax collector. Mary Magdalene was possessed by demons, and Paul supervised the murder of Christians.

However, God was able to use every one of these individuals because they were willing to be used for His purpose. God uses people with weaknesses and failures because those individuals must fully trust in God to allow Him to lead and teach. God's glory shines through us when we have nothing left of our own will and ego. Our shortcomings never disqualify us from being used by God. God's power is made perfect in our weakness (2 Corinthians 12:9).

If you want God to do more in your life then perhaps you need to submit more to Him. Ask God to forgive you of all of your un-confessed sins (name them to God) and surrender your entire life to God, saying, "Lord, send me. Use me. I am yours completely to fulfill Your will in my life." Then stand back and watch the mighty power of God change your life -- forever!

# Whether You Say "I Can" Or "I Can't" -- You Are Right!

*Acts 4:13*
*Now when they saw the boldness of Peter and John, and perceived that they were uneducated and untrained men, they marveled. And they realized that they had been with Jesus.*

Confidence is contagious. So is negativity. Think of a time when you have been around individuals who always doubted, complained about everything, and criticized everyone. How did that make you feel? Negative people carry a gray cloud above their heads wherever they go. They can turn the most festive atmosphere into a funeral in a short time.

Those with confidence believe they CAN -- no matter what the circumstances tell them. Confidence can change the outcome of a competitive contest, a battle, a marriage, or a life commitment. Christians should be the most confident, upbeat individuals that the world comes in contact with. Why? Because we have seen Jesus! Our confidence and hope is found in Christ. Many times Paul, Peter, and the other disciples testified before kings, the counsel of the Sanhedrin, or a hostile crowd. They amazed many with the gospel of Christ. These men were sometimes weak and timid, but they became powerful men of God. What made the difference? The message! They had the greatest message in the world and it gave them confidence to proclaim Christ to their world.

Surveys state that only 2% of Christians have shared their testimonies with someone else. Two percent witness and tell others of the life-changing message of Jesus Christ. Two percent! God have mercy on the Christian who does not share the good news! Many say I can't witness, I'm afraid of rejection, I'm embarrassed. If a man was in a burning building and you could share with him the way to get out of the building safely, would you? Would you be too frightened that he might reject your warning? Would you be embarrassed that you spoke up? How hard would you beg and plead with the man to come to safety?

Even if he were in the next room unaware of the fire and stated that he didn't feel like he was in danger, would you warn him anyway? I believe most people would without hesitation.

You might feel like an ordinary person with no special talent or gifts, but when you speak the gospel to others, they do not see you -- they see the message of Jesus. The Word of God is sharper than any two-edged sword and will pierce the hearts of men. The Holy Spirit will do the real work in the hearts of people; all you have to do is share your faith. We might not see immediate acceptance of what we share, but the Holy Spirit will continue to speak. This is why we are learning the scriptures to use in sharing the message of salvation, hope, encouragement, and deliverance.

Whether you say you can or you can't -- you're right!

# The Holy of Holies Is Now Open To All

*Matthew 27:51*
*Then, behold, the veil of the temple was torn in two from top to bottom;*
*and the earth quaked, and the rocks were split,*

The tabernacle of God was the place where the children of Israel went to worship God. This is where they would bring and offer their sacrifices unto the Lord. There was the outer court, the holy place, and the holy of holies. Only the high priest was allowed into the holy of holies to offer the sacrifice of atonement unto God for the entire nation of Israel. There was a large, thick curtain that separated the holy place from the holy of holies. When the high priest entered the holy of holies, he had to be completely clean of sin before entering or else he would drop dead. The other priests would tie a rope around the leg of the high priest before he entered the holy of holies. Why? If the high priest were to drop dead, they would need a way to get him out of that special place without going inside.

When Christ died on the cross, something amazing and wonderful happened. The curtain that separated the holy place from the holy of holies was torn in two, from top to bottom. This signified physically the work that Christ accomplished on the cross spiritually. Man no longer had to have a high priest to go before the throne of God for him, but he became able to go before God himself and seek God for his own forgiveness of sin! Hebrews 4:16 says, "So let us come boldly to the throne of our gracious God. There we will receive His mercy, and we will find grace to help us when we need it most." Jesus made a way for us all to approach the throne of God, to go into the spiritual holy of holies, and seek the face of God.

Have you made your visit with God today?

# God Listens!

James 5:16
*Confess your trespasses to one another, and pray for one another, that you may be healed. The effective, fervent prayer of a righteous man avails much.*

I have seen many miracles in my life. My grandfather, Rev. Buell Pitts, was an evangelist and a prayer warrior for God. I attended many of his revival services and witnessed many healing miracles. I saw people get out of wheelchairs and walk, blind eyes open, those with broken bones take off their casts and leave them at the altar. People with cancer were healed, and their healings were subsequently confirmed by their own physicians. My grandmother was deaf in one ear and she regained her hearing, along with healing from a crippling kind of arthritis. My sister was healed of a serious case of childhood rheumatic fever. All of these services were held in small rural churches with no cameras, no reporters, no self-promoting agenda, and a strong belief that God can do anything.

Why was my grandfather used so mightily by the Lord? I believe it was because he was a man of prayer and faith. If you want to be used of God, commit yourself to Him. If you want to be used mightily of God you must walk with Him daily and spend time in prayer and fasting. I know my grandfather completed at least three forty-day fasts before God, and it was during the times when God blessed his ministry with signs and wonders.

There are three components, according to this scripture, to seeing great results from God. First, the prayer must be effectual or effective. Pray with purpose. Wrestle with God! Challenge God with His Word and pray the scriptures. Know what you want from God and have faith that God will honor your prayer and your faith.

Second, your prayers must be fervent. Seek God and continue seeking God. Do not let go or give up. Just as you must come to Him with purpose, you must not leave without an answer. Tarry before the Lord and petition, praise, and proclaim the victory before leaving the presence of the Lord.

Third, you must be righteous before God. You must have a clean heart and a right spirit before the Lord. The scriptures state that Elijah asked for the heavens to be closed and not rain for three years and six months, and it did not rain. When he prayed again for the heavens to release the rain, it did rain.

It takes sacrifice and dedication to have the ear of God. But you will see a move of God like never before in your life if you fulfill the three requirements of James 5:16.

# Then Jesus . . .

*John 6:11*
*And Jesus took the loaves, and when He had given thanks He distributed*
*them to the disciples, and the disciples to those sitting down; and likewise*
*of the fish, as much as they wanted.*

Two fish and five loaves -- that doesn't sound like much if you're trying
to feed thousands of people. Most would say impossible. The disciples
were even wondering how they were going to feed all of the hungry
people. One little boy had a sack lunch of two fish and five loaves of
bread. Andrew brought him to Jesus and explained what the boy had,
and then asked Jesus, "What is this compared to so many people?"

*Then Jesus.* God asks us to give to Him whatever it is that we have. *Then
Jesus.* He will take the small beginning that we offer and do something
miraculous with it. *Then Jesus.* So many say I have nothing to offer.
What kind of difference could my little amount make? All God asks is
that we give Him what we have and *then Jesus.*

-- Then Jesus said to the Roman officers, "Go home; because you
believed, it has happened." (Matthew 8:13)

-- Then Jesus said to the woman, "Your sins are forgiven." (Luke 7:48)

-- Then Jesus placed his hands on the man's eyes again, and his eyes
were opened. (Mark 8:25)

-- Then Jesus shouted, "Lazarus, come forth!" (John 11:43)

-- Then Jesus rebuked the demon in the boy and it left him. (Matthew
17:18)

All it takes is a little faith, a little talent, a little money, a little effort, a
little compassion, a little obedience, and THEN JESUS!

# Jesus Wept

*John 11:35*
*Jesus wept.*

The shortest verse in the Bible: Jesus wept. Jesus went to Mary when he heard of the death of Lazarus. She was very upset and said to Jesus, "Lord, if you had been here, my brother would not have died." The scriptures also say when He saw Mary weeping that He groaned in His spirit and was troubled. Why? Jesus knew He could and was going to raise him from the dead.

I believe Jesus was showing compassion. He loved Lazarus but He loved Mary as well. He was giving comfort, understanding the pain of losing a loved one, and letting people know how to support each other. The Jews said, "See how He loved him!"

Jesus said to Mary, "If you believe, you will see the glory of God." Jesus then called Lazarus forth and Lazarus came out of the tomb alive.

Jesus weeps at death. Humans were never made to die. But sin came into our lives and brought forth a physical death. Jesus also does not want to see anyone die a spiritual death. Christ gave Himself to defeat death and the grave so no man would have to be robbed of his godly inheritance.

Accept the gift of God today and you will have eternal life with He who conquered death and the grave!

# Filthy Pig In A Suit

*1 Samuel 16:7*
*But the Lord said to Samuel, "Do not look at his appearance or at the height of his stature, because I have refused him. For the Lord does not see as man sees; for man looks at the outward appearance, but the Lord looks at the heart."*

Too many times Christians get too worried about the outward appearance. No shorts, no tattoos, no long hair, no jewelry, no going to certain places, etc. Legalism.

If you take a pig that has been wallowing in mud and put him in a suit, what do you have? A filthy pig in a suit. Take a man with an impure heart who rejects Christ but goes to church, has a nice haircut, shaven, no tattoos, talks religious jargon, and smiles a lot. Put this man into a nice $500 suit and what do you have? A filthily-inward man in a $500 suit. He might look nice but he is of no use to God's work. You can fool men but you cannot fool God.

God told Samuel to go look for Saul's replacement to be king. Samuel went to Jesse the Bethlehemite. Jesse called his sons before Samuel to see which one would be anointed of God to replace Saul. Samuel saw Eliab and said, "Surely, this is the one." He was tall, good looking, and had a great physical presence. But God said, "Do not look at his appearance as his physical stature, because I have refused him. For the Lord does not see man as man sees, for a man looks at the outward appearance but the Lord looks at the heart."

With God, it is what's inside that counts. David wrote in Psalms 51,"Create in me a clean heart, O God." Ask God to cleanse your heart today so His anointing might rest upon you for great works.

# Fear The Right Things

*Proverbs 1:7*
*The fear of the Lord is the beginning of knowledge, But fools despise wisdom and instruction.*

My mother had a bad experience with rats when she was little. The word rat doesn't describe the animal that she encountered. In the city of New Orleans they have wharf rats that can grow to be larger than cats. These rats would rather eat you than run from you! To this date, she has a phobia of any rat, hamster, squirrel, or other rodent. When I was young, one of her co-workers heard about her phobia and wanted to prank her. He didn't realize how serious it was but found out very quickly when he put a rat in a box for her to open and she fainted dead away. It scared everyone around her and they never pulled that prank again. Even now she cannot even watch a cartoon rat like in "Ratatouille."

What are you afraid of? Rats, bats, snakes, spiders, airplanes, heights, caves, being buried alive? Perhaps you are afraid of losing your job, your family, or your life. Some are afraid of being poor, unpopular, disliked, or irrelevant. Ninety-eight percent of Christians are afraid to share their faith with others. I say that because surveys state that only 2% of Christians are active in sharing their faith with others.

But I have news for the 98% and the unchurched. You had better fear the Lord above all others. The scriptures ask why fear the one who can kill the body? (Matthew 10:28) Rather, fear the one who can condemn the body and the soul. That would be God. To fear the Lord is the beginning of knowledge and wisdom.

God is love and He does love us, but He is also righteous and must punish sin. He has made a way for us to be saved from the consequences of sin. Be smart and fear the Lord. Accept Him today. Tell others of His saving grace.

It is better to be rejected by men than lose your place with God.

# Two Is Better Than One

*Matthew 18: 19,20*
*Again I say to you that if two of you agree on earth concerning anything that*
*they ask, it will be done for them by My Father in heaven. For where two or*
*three are gathered together in My name, I am there in the midst of them."*

In the old covenant, Moses' Covenant, two to three witnesses were
required to bring charges against anyone. Obviously, the more witnesses
who stated the same thing, the more credibility given to their word. In
like manner, Christ is saying if two believers agree on a request and ask
God, it will be done for them. Christ affirms that when there are two
to three believers gathered together in His name, He promises to be in
the midst of them.

There is power in unity. It is good to get those of like faith to agree with
you, pray with you, petition God together, and join forces in seeking
God. If we could get the church together for corporate prayer then I
believe we would see a mighty move of God again!

This passage is also talking about having unity in the body of Christ.
When a believer has done wrong in the body of Christ, He shows us
how to deal with the conflict wisely:

1.  Approach the offending party alone (v. 15).
2.  Confront the sin and hopefully receive resolution (v. 15).
3.  If the issue is not resolved, take one or two more with you as
    witnesses (v. 16).
4.  Get the facts straight and seek a resolution (v. 16).
5.  If no resolution, take before the body of Christ (v. 17).
6.  Set forth options for the offender if he listens to the body of
    Christ (v. 17).
7.  If not, release the offending party from the Church (v. 17).

Christ will support the decisions of the godly and He promises to always
be present when we gather in His name.

# There Will Be Doubters In The Last Days

*2 Peter 3:9*
*The Lord is not slack concerning His promise, as some count slackness, but is longsuffering toward us, not willing that any should perish but that all should come to repentance.*

The believers of the early church truly thought that Christ would return in their generation. They eagerly sought for His return and worked tirelessly to save as many as possible with the gospel of Christ.

We are now 2000 years closer to the return of Jesus Christ. The dispensation of Grace, or the Church Age, has already lasted longer than any other dispensational age of the world. The believers of the church today must remain vigilant and watchful for the coming of Christ! The Bible warns us that in the last days there will be those who ask, "Where is the promise of His coming? Why does He wait?" They say, "Maybe He will not return as foretold."

From the earliest time I can remember, my parents and grandparents would say, "Jesus is coming soon!" I didn't want to miss His return, but the longer it took the more I lost my passion and state of watchfulness. Time brought a slacking attitude.

But this verse says, "The Lord is not slack concerning His promise, as some count slackness, but is longsuffering toward us, not willing that any should perish but that all should come to repentance."

The only reason Christ is waiting is so more people will accept Him as Lord and Savior. He does not want any to perish. But there will come a day when He will return for His church and we will be taken to be with Him forever. Tell someone about the Lord today!

# Smile, You're On God's Camera!

*2 Corinthians 5:10*
*For we must all appear before the judgment seat of Christ, that each one may receive the things done in the body, according to what he has done, whether good or bad.*

How many of you remember the old television show *Candid Camera*? This show would set up people to be pranked or see how they would respond to a situation, not knowing they were on camera. At the end of the sequence, someone would yell to them, "Smile! You're on *Candid Camera!*" It was funny and sometimes not so funny to see how people responded and then discovered they were being filmed.

This verse is our warning! We are being watched and recorded every second of our life! Every believer will have to stand before Christ at the judgment seat to see what we have done in this life, good or bad. That should make all of us reconsider our behavior. There is no hiding from God. There are no do-overs. We will be rewarded based on our obedience to God during our lives while on earth.

The good news is this judgment is for believers only. So if you made it to the judgment seat of Christ, you have accepted Christ as your Lord and Savior.

The great white throne judgment has been reserved for those individuals and nations who have rejected Christ.

So, wherever you go, whatever you do, whatever you think -- remember, you're on God's camera!

# The Discipline of Self-Discipline

*1 Corinthian 6:19*
*Or do you not know that your body is the temple of the Holy Spirit who is in you, whom you have from God, and you are not your own?*

Beep! Beep! Beep! Oh, how I hate that sound, especially at 4:30 in the morning! Rise and shine, time to work out, baby! My wife is faithful to get up and work out every day. I'm not as faithful. I know I need to exercise, but my bed feels so good. "Come on now, get your head out of bed, you ain't listening to what I said," she says playfully. My wife is a certified personal trainer so I have no excuse not to be in good shape. She will tell me, "Come on now, you need to take care of my body for me." Your body? She's actually right.

The scriptures say that we are not our own. We are bought with a price. Our body is the temple of the Holy Spirit, who is in us at all times. The Holy Spirit was given to us by God to reside in us and to guide us. With God's help, we must be self-disciplined for many reasons.

First, we are to glorify God with our body and our spirit. All that we are should be to the glory of God. Every word, action, and thought should give Him honor. Secondly, our body belongs to our spouse. The scripture says when a man and a woman are joined together, they become one (I Corinthians :15-17). Our body represents not only God but our spouse as well. Thirdly, our body belongs to the body of Christ. We are to serve the body of Christ and use the gifts the Lord has given us to minister.

Are you taking care of the temple of the Holy Spirit? Are you allowing defiled objects into the temple? We must preserve and strengthen our body, mind, soul, and spirit every day to be our best for God, our spouse, and the body of Christ.

Beep! Beep! Beep! Here we go again. Rise and shine!

# The Service of Serving

*Romans 15:1*
*We then who are strong ought to bear with the scruples of the weak, and not to please ourselves.*

Servanthood -- when is the last time you heard a message preached on this subject? Only the mature can be a servant. Only the spirit-led can set aside their desires and needs for the continued growth of the worker brother or sister in Christ. In Romans 14:14-23, Paul is telling us about the law of love. He is stating here that nothing is unclean in itself, but he sees that through his maturity in Christ. The law of love also states that we must "pursue the things which make for peace and the things by which one may edify another." He is referring to how to treat our brothers and sisters in Christ.

In Romans 15:1-6, he gives us six ways to have a servant's heart.

Verse 1: We are to please others and not just ourselves. Do not do something simply because it is lawful if it might cause a brother to stumble.

Verse 2: We are to edify others. Encourage your church family and push them toward greater works for Christ.

Verse 3: If wronged, we are to forgive. This is the example of Christ -- to forgive all, even when they were obviously wrong.

Verse 4: Look to the Word of God as our example. The scriptures were written so we can learn and have hope through patience and comfort.

Verse 5: We are to learn from one another. Remain teachable and seek to grow whenever possible.

Verse 6: Seek to be like-minded. Pursue lasting, godly relationships and pray that your unity will glorify God.

We are definitely our brother's keeper!

# Baby Steps

*Psalms 37:23, 24*
*The steps of a good man are ordered by the Lord, And He delights in his way. Though he fall, he shall not be utterly cast down; For the Lord upholds him with His hand.*

Those who have children will be able to relate to what I am about to say. Do you remember when your children were just learning to walk? They wanted to be so independent, yet you still wanted to assist them and guide them to make sure they didn't fall and get hurt. My daughter, Carissa, wanted to go! She would take off trying to walk, laughing, having fun, and then thump! She would hit the ground. She would look at me with this "what happened?" kind of look. I would pick her up and she would be off walking again. I would hold her hand while she was walking, and she was so happy and proud! I would let go but be standing right beside her with my hands ready to catch her at any moment. I'm sure all of you can remember the early days with your children, or you may be experiencing them right now.

God orders the steps of His children. God loves watching His children grow, mature, and learn to walk in His ways. He is right there holding our hands, guiding us until we can walk on our own. Once He lets go, He knows we will stumble, maybe even fall down. But He is there to tend to us, love us, and pick us up to walk again. As a proud parent, He will always be watching and ready to intervene when needed.

God also ordains our steps. In other words, He sets our path and course in life. If we will only trust our heavenly Father to be our compass in life and simply trust and obey His will, we will find true happiness and contentment in His ways.

Trust and obey
For there's no other way
To be happy in Jesus
Than to trust and obey.

# Blessings Or Curses -- Our Choice

*Deuteronomy 28:1*
*"Now it shall come to pass, if you diligently obey the voice of the Lord your God, to observe carefully all His commandments which I command you today, that the Lord your God will set you high above all nations of the earth."*

Moses was a mighty man of God. He was not a perfect man but he sought the Lord and His guidance about how to lead the children of Israel. During this time, the Israelites were preparing to enter into their promised land. Many did not see the miracles in Egypt. They had grown up in the wilderness. Moses realized that this generation needed fresh inspiration to continue serving God. Moses set forth a vision to the children of Israel stating the blessing associated with serving God. Not just for the nation but for families and individuals. He also set forth the curses for disobedience unto the Lord. He reminded them to grow in the Lord, learn His Word, be obedient, and remain in the favor of God. Moses gave them two options -- serve God and be blessed, or disobey God and be cursed.

America had the blessing of God from its birth. The founding fathers recognized God as their leader and commander-in-chief. George Washington, Abraham Lincoln, and others stated that America must continue to serve the true God to be blessed. For 200 years we were blessed because of our obedience.

Now we are being cursed. America has turned from serving God as a country. We kicked God out of our schools and universities. We have taken the commandments off the walls of our courtrooms. We kill thousands of babies every day. We curse the name of God for fun. Every religion is accepted except Christianity. I just read where New Orleans has outlawed witnessing or preaching the gospel in the French Quarter from sundown to sunrise. You can do every ungodly thing imaginable, but you cannot talk about Jesus! The state of Delaware just passed a law forbidding parents from spanking their children (because it causes physical pain). That is the point of discipline, isn't it? Parents caught disciplining their children with any physical pain can go to jail for up to two years! A pastor cannot say a prayer at a football game, but a national political party can have a two hour Muslim prayer service to open up their convention.

America needs to repent of its wicked ways and turn back to God! Christians need to stop seeking preachers will tickle their ears. We must find a minister who will preach a true message from God. You and I need to proclaim the message of the law, repentance, grace, and salvation before it is too late!

God has set His principles in motion. Seek the Lord and serve Him and you will be blessed. But if you turn from God, everything you own and know will be cursed. Read Deuteronomy 27:1-28:68 for the specific blessings and curses of God.

God have mercy on America! We must return to our first love for Him.

# Remember Faith?

*Hebrews 11:6*
*But without faith it is impossible to please Him, for he who comes to God must believe that He is, and that He is a rewarder of those who diligently seek Him.*

Faith. There probably hasn't been a more punished or misused word in the Bible. Just because there have been some to abuse the word, use it for their own glory, doesn't mean that it still is not a valuable part of God's toolbox. Simply put, without faith it is impossible to please God. Faith is a basic building block of relationship with God. Many of us use our faith to believe God will pay a bill, save a loved one, or even fill our gas tank when we need it.

Remember Joshua? He was one of the spies who went into their promised land to check it out. He and his friend Caleb said, "No problem, God will lead us into the land and will give it to us" (Numbers 14:7-9). However, the other ten spies said, "we can never overtake them for there are giants in the land." The people of Israel wasted forty years for their unbelief.

God has new lands for us to conquer as well. We must have faith and go forth as Joshua. He became the leader of Israel after Moses sent forth to claim the land that God had promised them. Joshua knew there would be battles, but he also knew God would fight the battles with them! We must believe God for the impossible, ask for the impossible, and then act to receive the impossible. Have the audacity to ask something of God that has never been done before.

Joshua did. During a battle against the Amorites, Joshua attacked first. As they fought, the Amorite army retreated, and the Bible says that God hurled large hailstones down on them from the sky (Numbers 14:11). Wow, can you imagine? Then as the sun was setting for the day, Joshua had a now-or-never approach to defeating his enemies -- he prayed and asked God to make the sun stand still. Can you imagine ever asking such a thing from God? Who does he think he is to ask God to stop the sun and to hold it in place? What are we asking God to do in our lives? God gave Joshua exactly what he prayed for and had faith to believe that God would do -- the sun stood still! (Numbers 14:13-14).

Do you now understand the power of the God we serve? He created the sun so he can stop it at will. I have so many questions about how He did this, but I digress. God honors faith. He answered the prayer of Joshua because he truly believed that God would answer. "You have not because you ask not." God wants us to challenge Him with our faith. Because when we do we are actually challenging ourselves and stretching our faith.

But remember, high rewards have high costs. God will demand true repentance, faithfulness, and obedience to His Word and will. Set your vision so high that it has to be God in the middle of it to be fulfilled. Sure, there will be battles, temptation to quit, or unbelief to slither in, but reaffirm the vision, state it to God, and keep diligently working to put faith in action.

God needs people like Joshua today who will have unwavering faith in the awesome, life-changing power of the Almighty!

# I Am Who I Am

*Exodus 3:14*
*And God said to Moses, "I AM WHO I AM." And He said, "Thus you shall say to the children of Israel, 'I AM has sent me to you.*

Do you really know God? Do you really know who He is? God says, "I am who I am." There is no changing God to meet our expectations or desires. We need to learn Him just as He is and always will be.

**God is Holy**. He is set apart. He is perfect. To say, "Holy, holy, holy" is to say that God is perfectly set apart with nothing and no one to compare Him to. That is the definition of "holy."

**God is Eternal**. Everything had a beginning; everything had a start date. Everything but God! God has always been and always will be. You and I cannot fully comprehend this with our finite mind. Imagine we are thimbles and God is an ocean. Just because our thimble gets full of water in no way means we have experienced the fullness of the ocean. "But you remain the same, and your years will never end" (Psalms 102:12).

**God is All-Knowing**. God knows everything about you, about all of us. What we think, our desires, what we are planning, and even how we will respond to Him. Nothing can hide from God, not the darkness, and not even a child in his mother's womb (Hebrews 4:13). Nothing in all creation is hidden from God's sight.

**God is All-Powerful**. All things were created by Him and for Him. So many believe He was created to meet our needs, answer our demands, and do our bidding! We were created for His pleasure. (Colossians 1:16).

# Another Counselor

*John 14:16*
*And I will pray the Father, and He will give you another Helper, that He may abide with you forever--*

The Greek word for another means "another that is just like the first." Jesus was trying to tell His disciples that the Father would send another one and He would be just like Jesus! This counselor was coming to live inside of us. What is being said here is we have a counselor, the mind of Christ, living inside of us to be our advisor, guide, and comforter.

Imagine receiving perfect and flawless truth all the time. We have a member of the trinity -- the Holy Spirit -- inside of us all of the time. Shouldn't that make us different than those in the world? No wonder the world expects more of us if we profess to have God living inside us.

What if I told the world that a god of football had come to dwell inside me. I would be expected to play football better than anyone else, run faster, jump higher, throw farther, and score more than anyone else. It would be expected because I would have power that other players did not have.

As a Christian, we have the Holy Spirit within us. We need to love more, forgive more, have more faith, care for the less fortunate more, and have more joy than those who do not know Christ. If we do not, why would unbelievers want anything to do with our God?

The Holy Spirit lives inside of us, so we should ask Him to help us change our world for Christ!

# *Victory!*

*1 Corinthians 15:51, 52*
*Behold, I tell you a mystery: We shall not all sleep, but we shall all be changed--in a moment, in the twinkling of an eye, at the last trumpet. For the trumpet will sound, and the dead will be raised incorruptible, and we shall be changed.*

All through the Word of God we see stories of tribulation, sin, and failure, including the Adam nature, and Satan's victory in the Garden of Eden. There are also temporary victories for the faithful, but because of the defeat in the Garden, death took over victory. Or did it? Of course not! Death reigned for only a moment. Paul closes the book of Romans with a reminder that we have absolute victory if we are faithful to the very end. We have the same guarantee, and that should encourage and inspire us to fulfill our mission in Christ.

We cannot inherit the kingdom of God in this flesh and blood body. But Paul shares with us a mystery, something that was previously unknown. We will not sleep (die) but we will all be changed in a moment, quickly, in an instant, in the twinkling of an eye! Now, that is fast. This will take place at the sound of the last trumpet. The dead in Christ will be raised and changed to immortal first, then those who are still living will be changed from mortal to immortal. Praise God!

Then the Word of God will ring out:
"Death is swallowed up in victory.
O' death, where is your sting?
O' grave, where is victory?"

The sting of death and its deliverer the law will have been defeated once and for all through our Lord Jesus Christ.

Remember, be steadfast and know that your labor is never in vain when working for the Lord! I pray I will see you on the streets of gold one day!